**OPPOSING
VIEWPOINTS®
SERIES**

Space Exploration

Other Books of Related Interest:

Opposing Viewpoints Series

Endangered Oceans

The Environment

Robotic Technology

Scientific Research

At Issue Series

Are Natural Disasters Increasing?

Can Glacier and Ice Melt Be Reversed?

Drones

Hybrid and Electric Cars

Wind Farms

Current Controversies Series

Global Warming

Oil Spills

Pollution

"Congress shall make no law ... abridging the freedom of speech, or of the press."

First Amendment to the US Constitution

The basic foundation of our democracy is the First Amendment guarantee of freedom of expression. The Opposing Viewpoints series is dedicated to the concept of this basic freedom and the idea that it is more important to practice it than to enshrine it.

OPPOSING
VIEWPOINTS®
SERIES

Space Exploration

Michael Ruth, Book Editor

GREENHAVEN PRESS
A part of Gale, Cengage Learning

GALE
CENGAGE Learning·

Farmington Hills, Mich • San Francisco • New York • Waterville, Maine
Meriden, Conn • Mason, Ohio • Chicago

Judy Galens, *Manager, Frontlist Acquisitions*

For more information, contact:
Greenhaven Press
27500 Drake Rd.
Farmington Hills, MI 48331-3535
Or you can visit our Internet site at gale.cengage.com

For product information and technology assistance, contact us at

Gale Customer Support, 1-800-877-4253
For permission to use material from this text or product, submit all requests online at
www.cengage.com/permissions

Further permissions questions can be emailed to permissionrequest@cengage.com

Articles in Greenhaven Press anthologies are often edited for length to meet page requirements. In addition, original titles of these works are changed to clearly present the main thesis and to explicitly indicate the author's opinion. Every effort is made to ensure that Greenhaven Press accurately reflects the original intent of the authors. Every effort has been made to trace the owners of copyrighted material.

LIBRARY OF CONGRESS CATALOGING-IN-PUBLICATION DATA

Space exploration / Michael Ruth, book editor.
    pages cm. -- (Opposing viewpoints)
Includes bibliographical references and index.
ISBN 978-0-7377-7562-4 (hardcover) -- ISBN 978-0-7377-7563-1 (pbk.)
1. Outer space--Exploration--Public opinion. I. Ruth, Michael, editor.
TL793.S659 2016
629.43'5--dc23
                    2015029838

Printed in the United States of America
1 2 3 4 5   20 19 18 17 16

Contents

Chapter 3: What Are the Politics of Space Exploration?

Chapter 4: What Is the Science Behind Space Exploration?

Why Consider
Opposing Viewpoints?

"The only way in which a human being can make some approach to knowing the whole of a subject is by hearing what can be said about it by persons of every variety of opinion and studying all modes in which it can be looked at by every character of mind. No wise man ever acquired his wisdom in any mode but this."

John Stuart Mill

In our media-intensive culture it is not difficult to find differing opinions. Thousands of newspapers and magazines and dozens of radio and television talk shows resound with differing points of view. The difficulty lies in deciding which opinion to agree with and which "experts" seem the most credible. The more inundated we become with differing opinions and claims, the more essential it is to hone critical reading and thinking skills to evaluate these ideas. Opposing Viewpoints books address this problem directly by presenting stimulating debates that can be used to enhance and teach these skills. The varied opinions contained in each book examine many different aspects of a single issue. While examining these conveniently edited opposing views, readers can develop critical thinking skills such as the ability to compare and contrast authors' credibility, facts, argumentation styles, use of persuasive techniques, and other stylistic tools. In short, the Opposing Viewpoints Series is an ideal way to attain the higher-level thinking and reading skills so essential in a culture of diverse and contradictory opinions.

In addition to providing a tool for critical thinking, Opposing Viewpoints books challenge readers to question their own strongly held opinions and assumptions. Most people form their opinions on the basis of upbringing, peer pressure, and personal, cultural, or professional bias. By reading carefully balanced opposing views, readers must directly confront new ideas as well as the opinions of those with whom they disagree. This is not to argue simplistically that everyone who reads opposing views will—or should—change his or her opinion. Instead, the series enhances readers' understanding of their own views by encouraging confrontation with opposing ideas. Careful examination of others' views can lead to the readers' understanding of the logical inconsistencies in their own opinions, perspective on why they hold an opinion, and the consideration of the possibility that their opinion requires further evaluation.

Evaluating Other Opinions

To ensure that this type of examination occurs, Opposing Viewpoints books present all types of opinions. Prominent spokespeople on different sides of each issue as well as well-known professionals from many disciplines challenge the reader. An additional goal of the series is to provide a forum for other, less known, or even unpopular viewpoints. The opinion of an ordinary person who has had to make the decision to cut off life support from a terminally ill relative, for example, may be just as valuable and provide just as much insight as a medical ethicist's professional opinion. The editors have two additional purposes in including these less known views. One, the editors encourage readers to respect others' opinions—even when not enhanced by professional credibility. It is only by reading or listening to and objectively evaluating others' ideas that one can determine whether they are worthy of consideration. Two, the inclusion of such viewpoints encourages the important critical thinking skill of objectively evaluating an author's credentials and bias. This evaluation will illuminate an author's reasons for taking a particular stance on an issue and will aid in readers' evaluation of the author's ideas.

It is our hope that these books will give readers a deeper understanding of the issues debated and an appreciation of the complexity of even seemingly simple issues when good and honest people disagree. This awareness is particularly important in a democratic society such as ours in which people enter into public debate to determine the common good. Those with whom one disagrees should not be regarded as enemies but rather as people whose views deserve careful examination and may shed light on one's own.

Thomas Jefferson once said that "difference of opinion leads to inquiry, and inquiry to truth." Jefferson, a broadly educated man, argued that "if a nation expects to be ignorant and free . . . it expects what never was and never will be." As individuals and as a nation, it is imperative that we consider the opinions of others and examine them with skill and discernment. The Opposing Viewpoints series is intended to help readers achieve this goal.

David L. Bender and Bruno Leone,
Founders

Introduction

"From the dawn of man until very recently, humans have been Earthbound, unable to reach even the clouds—let alone space. It's only within the last hundred years or so that the advent of manned flight and rocket ships has made the heavens attainable."

—*"Space Exploration,"*
NationalGeographic.com

Conversations about space exploration in the early twenty-first century have focused on a variety of developing space industries not thought possible in any previous time or place. Government-sponsored organizations such as the National Aeronautics and Space Administration (NASA) continue to improve technologies, including various roaming satellites, probes, and Mars rovers, for their own space missions. However, the private space industry—with its cost-effective, more efficient hardware—is primarily responsible for a number of forward leaps in the development of human space exploration. The principal areas of development—space tourism, asteroid mining, perpetual thrust drives, and space colonization—all have been advanced and made famous chiefly by private space companies.

The idea of colonizing other planets has become an especially relevant and contentious subject with the rise of Elon Musk's private aerospace company Space Exploration Technologies Corporation, commonly referred to as SpaceX. Since its founding in 2002, the corporation has made international headlines mainly for developing its own reusable line of rockets, the Falcon 9, which it has employed, with varying degrees of success, to run contractual resupply missions to the International Space Station (ISS) for NASA. Aside from these rocket launches, however, SpaceX has garnered just as much attention for Musk's enthusiasm for taking human beings to live permanently on Mars. He has claimed since the company's founding that he is determined to make humans an interplanetary species.

Musk said in an interview with Business Insider that his obsession with establishing a sustainable human residence on Mars began when, as a young man, he read popular science fiction works such as Isaac Asimov's Foundation series. The Foundation series chronicles the troubles that follow the collapse of a great galactic empire. Musk stated that the series taught him that most civilizations eventually fall and that this destiny is likely awaiting the human race. What would people do if Earth becomes an unsustainable home? Musk asked himself. His answer was to become interplanetary, to create the capability not only to transport human beings to Mars but also to establish long-term dwellings for them there. Thus SpaceX, the manifestation of Musk's vision for humanity, was born, and Musk himself repeatedly expressed his desire to live out his final years on the red planet.

The ambition to make human beings a spacefaring race has been supported by some and derided by others. The idea did not originate with Musk; in the twenty-first century, as Musk was endeavoring toward Mars with SpaceX, scientists at NASA already had begun researching and conceptualizing the human colonization of Venus, which, they claimed, would involve the installation of floating cities above the planet's hostile surface. Despite this, scientists roundly criticized Musk's lofty intentions of traveling to Mars and refuted his assertions about the effort's viability. Common counterarguments to Musk's reasoning mention the red planet's extreme cold, lack of atmosphere (which would protect a human population from cancer-causing cosmic radiation), frequent dust storms, and the exorbitant price of building strong, permanent settlements. Nevertheless, Musk pressed on, directing all of SpaceX's work toward Mars and ignoring outside disapproval of his plans.

One point on which Musk and the scientific community could generally agree was that Earth ultimately will become a hostile environment for humans. Scientists contend that the reasons for this inevitability are numerous. One threat to Earth's future is impact by an asteroid. About a third of the thousand-mile-wide asteroids that will drift near Earth's orbit over the next several hundred million years will eventually strike the planet with the force of a thousand nuclear explosions. The result of such an impact would be the near total destruction of Earth.

Another guaranteed threat to life on Earth is the expansion of the sun that will occur in about a billion years, as the star's supply of hydrogen begins to deplete. As the sun grows, its temperature will increase dramatically, causing oceans and all other water on Earth to boil and evaporate. Without water, all living things on the planet will die in quick succession. Finally, Musk said, if the natural environment does not kill off the human race, people themselves will, either through overconsumption of Earth's natural resources or global nuclear war. Becoming interplanetary is not only achievable, Musk asserted, but also necessary to avoid the extinction of humanity.

Opposing Viewpoints: Space Exploration examines the issues currently facing the international community's forays into space. Authors of greatly diverse opinions discuss these issues in chapters titled "What Is the Role of Space Exploration in the Modern World?," "Where in Space Should Humans Explore?," "What Are the Politics of Space Exploration?," and "What Is the Science Behind Space Exploration?"

 OPPOSING
VIEWPOINTS®
SERIES

What Is the Role of Space Exploration in the Modern World?

Chapter Preface

Two key events have marked the status of Western space exploration in the early twenty-first century: the end of the National Aeronautics and Space Administration's (NASA's) manned space shuttle program and the near simultaneous rise of human spaceflight by private enterprises. Among the numerous corporations attempting to develop space tourism— the ability to fly civilians into outer space for recreation—two in particular continually earn widespread media attention for their preeminence in technological development: the American company SpaceX and Britain's Virgin Galactic. Although those in the scientific community have applauded both companies for their many successes, an especially disastrous 2014 testing accident by Virgin Galactic also made scientists note the inherent dangers of sending humans into space.

The incident took place in October 2014, as Virgin Galactic was testing its VSS *Enterprise* SpaceShipTwo spaceplane over its launch facility in California's Mojave Desert. Two pilots, Peter Siebold and Michael Alsbury, were aboard the plane, preparing to take direct control of the craft as soon as it was deployed from its mothership, WhiteKnightTwo, which had carried *Enterprise* to cruising altitude. However, Alsbury had prematurely unlocked *Enterprise*'s movable tail, part of the plane's descent system. As a result, almost instantly upon deploying from WhiteKnightTwo, *Enterprise* began rapidly descending, breaking up in midair and plummeting to the ground below. While Siebold survived by ejecting from the plane, Alsbury died in the crash.

The event was a significant setback for Virgin Galactic's space tourism plans, as the company announced that it could take up to a year for the US federal government to complete its investigation of the crash. Meanwhile, media outlets began reporting that several public figures who had registered to be among the first passengers on Virgin's space tours had retracted their names and ticket payments soon after the *Enterprise* accident. Additionally, Virgin postponed its initial flight date of 2015 to an unspecified future date, during which time it would continue testing SpaceShipTwo from the Spaceport America launch site in New Mexico.

Alsbury's death raised the question of whether opening space simply for civilian tourism was worth its tremendous dangers. According to an article at Space.com, this sentiment was shared by Virgin Galactic founder Richard Branson, who publicly questioned whether the company's goals could be justified following the crash and fatality. He later visited the Mojave launch site, where, he claimed, the dedication of the crew reinvigorated his enthusiasm for the future of manned spaceflight. The worldwide public continues to debate the question.

The following chapter presents viewpoints on where space exploration fits into the twenty-first-century world. Topics discussed include human interstellar spaceflight, the funding of NASA, and the benefits and hazards of space tourism.

"There will come a time, then, when we must choose between a destiny among the stars or extinction."

Humanity Should Begin Planning for Interstellar Space Travel

Nelson Bridwell

Nelson Bridwell is a writer for SpaceNews. *In the following viewpoint, Bridwell argues that because planet Earth will not last forever, humans should begin planning now to establish permanent settlements among the stars. He suggests that people begin developing the technology to transport humans to another hospitable solar system, provided that they can comfortably survive the long trip there. In this way, Bridwell believes, the human race will not become extinct.*

As you read, consider the following questions:

1. What does Bridwell say will happen when the sun becomes 10 percent brighter than it is today?

Nelson Bridwell, "Op-Ed: To Be or Not To Be? Mankind's Exodus to the Stars," Spacenews.com, January 22, 2015. Copyright © 2015 Space News Inc. All rights reserved. Reproduced with permission.

2. What does Bridwell say should be the first goal of mankind's future space program?

3. What does Bridwell suggest should be the future of humanity's life on Mars and the moon?

Today, Earth is a very accommodating and hospitable place for us to live. Temperatures are just about right. There is more than enough oxygen for us to breathe. Pure drinking water falls from the skies. Food grows on trees. For what more could we ask?

These near ideal conditions are dependent upon our nearest star, the sun. Our understanding of solar physics and astronomical observations of other stars tells us that since its formation the sun has grown 30 percent brighter. Over the course of time, this increase in brightness will continue. It is projected that when it becomes only 10 percent brighter than today, the increased radiant energy reaching Earth will have vaporized the oceans, creating H_2O greenhouse conditions that will raise temperatures by several hundred degrees, killing off all plant and animal life.

Because the sun burns through 600 million tons of hydrogen per second, it has already consumed almost half of its hydrogen stockpile. Further down the road, after this supply of hydrogen has become depleted, the sun will become a red giant star, rapidly burning through its limited accumulation of helium. The brightness of the sun will dramatically increase in nearly a dozen outbursts over the course of a few thousand years, peaking at 10,000 times its current brightness and ballooning out to more than 250 times its current diameter, swallowing all of the inner planets, including Earth.

As the helium becomes exhausted, the sun will unleash its outer shell as a massive tsunami of particles and ionized gases that will sweep across the remaining solar system, forming a planetary nebula. Finally, the core of the sun will collapse, becoming a faint, tiny, white dwarf star that will slowly fade to black.

Although our home planet may be a paradise today, hundreds of millions of years into the future it will become a hell.

And billions of years later, it will cease to exist. There will come a time, then, when we must choose between a destiny among the stars or extinction. To be, or not to be? That will be the question.

Reasonable Survival Precautions

At this moment, we are not totally prepared to embark on an interstellar escape. Fortunately, we may have millions of years to develop the required technologies and marshal the enormous resources needed for a mass emigration to another solar system.

What are the beginning steps that we should take now in order to make sure that we will be ready when the time comes?

The first step is to make sure that everyone understands the unfortunate fate that awaits this lovely planet—and us if we fail to act. The potential extinction of the entire human race, no matter how far into the future, is no laughing matter.

The second step is to take reasonable precautions to guarantee that mankind will continue to thrive on this planet for millions of years. If the entire human race should perish tomorrow night, then starships will probably not be happening anytime soon. We should therefore minimize the risk that our future could be jeopardized by warfare, diseases or natural disasters.

There is a variety of precautions that we could take.

In theory, we could carefully screen our political and military leadership to disqualify mentally unbalanced, destructive or irresponsible individuals.

Will Orion Make Interstellar Space Travel Possible?

The U.S. National Aeronautics and Space Administration (NASA) has revealed that its latest Orion spacecraft is complete. Orion is expected to assist human travel into deep space such as Mars.

Humans have reached space and have also landed on the surface of the moon. Many scientists have long hoped to land on the surface of Mars, and it seems that the Orion spacecraft will help scientists achieve the dream. . . .

The Orion will initially be launched atop a Delta IV Heavy rocket. However, it is expected that future Orion launches will be on the Space Launch System (SLS), NASA's latest heavy-lift rocket.

NASA claims that the SLS is the most powerful rocket ever built, which will be capable of sending manned spacecraft to deep-space asteroids and possibly Mars. Various space agencies across the world including NASA have successfully launched their unmanned spacecraft to the red planet. However, no human has reached beyond the moon. . . .

Orion is ready for a test flight, but it remains to be seen how many more years it takes for man to actually land of the surface of the red planet.

Sumit Passary,
"NASA Orion Spacecraft May Make Interstellar
Space Travel Reality," Tech Times, November 1, 2014.

We could prepare compartmentalization procedures that could be implemented whenever a deadly epidemic threatens to rapidly spread throughout the world.

We could accelerate the search for near-Earth asteroids and comets in order to provide advanced warning of threats. And if required, we could assemble an arsenal of kinetic and/or thermonuclear warheads that could be used to deflect killer asteroids.

If worst comes to worst, we could construct underground shelters that would protect much of humanity from almost anything that nature (or man) could throw at us.

The third step is to align our space program to this long-term objective so that we will have the knowledge and technologies required to someday reach the stars and thrive, comfortably, when we arrive. A consistent direction, stable headcounts and affordable budgets will be essential to achieve such challenging long-term objectives. In order to be able to support this sustained effort, we will need a productive economy and an educated workforce.

The Importance of a Space Program

The first goal of our space program should be to conduct a search, using advanced telescopes, for the most promising nearby solar system for the future of mankind.

The second goal should be the development of closed-loop life-support technologies that can keep humanity alive and well on long interstellar voyages. These technologies also could be utilized on manned space missions to Mars and could even help [safeguard] humanity on this planet.

Because it is not at all likely that a warm, moist, green, oxygen-rich twin of Earth will be within our reach, the third goal must be learning how to live under less ideal conditions, such as on the moon. We should establish manned outposts on the moon and Mars where we can develop the expertise to efficiently manufacture everything that we need from local planetary materials. Over the course of hundreds of years, as these outposts grow, they will become second homes within this solar system for humanity.

The final and most challenging goal of our space program will be the development of interstellar spacecraft for transporting humanity to safer places when this solar system turns hostile. Although this will not require faster-than-light travel or other violations of physics, the development of this technology will not happen overnight. Because starships will not be ready to go for many centuries and interstellar voyages may last for thousands of years, we will want to get started sooner rather than later, initially allocating a small but steady fraction of the space budget to identify the most promising engineering approaches and performing early proof-of-concept experiments when affordable. The first application of this technology will be for unmanned interstellar probes that will conduct close-up reconnaissance of nearby solar systems.

Today we live in a culture that is so overly obsessed with the current moment that we are reluctant to think beyond the next few months or years. Perhaps our dystopian aversion to the future is a madness left over from the Cold War [nonviolent post–World War II conflict between the United States and the Soviet Union]. In any case, this stellar challenge will require us to begin seriously planning for our future. It should also provide us with a greater sense of purpose and a more positive outlook. Because concrete steps will be taken to ensure that really bad things will never happen, we can rest assured that the story of mankind, unlike the tragedy of Prince Hamlet, will not come to a premature end.

> *"By funding a space program, we inspire the next generation to enter the fields of science and engineering."*

NASA Should Continue to Receive Funding

CJ Miozzi

CJ Miozzi is a writer for the Escapist website. In the following viewpoint, Miozzi argues that the National Aeronautics and Space Administration (NASA) should continue to be federally funded because of its practical applications of technology to human society. The work done by NASA not only furthers space exploration but also encourages future generations to become involved in science and engineering. Miozzi contends that research and development conducted by NASA over the years has led to the advancement of science in general and to inventions used in everyday life, including ear thermometers, invisible dental braces, and satellite television. He concludes that the space program should continue to receive funding so the universe can be further explored and new discoveries can be made.

As you read, consider the following questions:

1. What percentage of the US federal budget does Miozzi say NASA receives?

2. How does Miozzi say some of the greatest inventions in human history have been produced?

3. What does Miozzi say exploring space shows the world about the human race?

A recent report from the U.S. National Research Council found that the public does not consider investing money in the space program a priority. This poses a problem for NASA [National Aeronautics and Space Administration], which, with its current level of funding, will never be able to undertake a massive endeavor like a manned mission to Mars.

Public apathy toward NASA, a lack of understanding of the benefits of a space program, and more pressing matters all lead people to ask: Is NASA worth funding at all? Couldn't that money be better spent working on the economy, homelessness, or the housing market?

That Level of Funding

A key misconception among Americans is the amount of government money that goes to the space program. Just how much funding does NASA receive, relative to other governmental departments? Probably not as much as you think.

In 2013. . .

- The Department of Justice received double the funding NASA received.

- The Department of Homeland Security received three times the funding.

- The Department of Education received four times the funding.

- The Department of Transportation received five times the funding.

- The Department of the Treasury received six times the funding.

- The Department of Defense, including the ongoing efforts of the Overseas Contingency Operations, received over 35 times the funding NASA received.

For the past few years, NASA's budget has accounted for roughly 0.5% of the total U.S. federal budget. 1966 marked the height of NASA's funding, when it received 4.41% of the total budget—nine times the relative budget it receives currently. In fact, 1963–1969 were the only years in history that NASA received over 2% of the total budget. And what was it able to accomplish with that level of funding? Oh, just a little historic event like *landing a man on the moon.*

But maybe you don't want your hard-earned tax dollars being put toward space shenanigans. Maybe you resent the fact that roughly $10—yes, a whopping $10—of your annual personal income tax goes to fund NASA. We have bigger problems to solve here on Earth; why allocate money to space exploration? What has NASA ever done for you?

I'm so glad you asked.

What Has NASA Done?

Research and development either led by NASA or effectuated through partnerships with NASA have led to inventions that have found everyday, practical use in our lives.

Those cordless tools in your cabinet? They evolved from technology developed from the Apollo lunar landing program. That ear thermometer that saves you an awkward rectal exam? Developed from the application of 30 years of experience in remote measurement of the temperatures of stars and planets. How long do your tires last? You can attribute 10,000 miles of their tread life to tire technology developed for Mars rovers.

Increasing NASA Funding Will Help America Advance

Reinvigorating space exploration in the United States will require not only boosting NASA's budget but also getting the public to understand how pushing the boundaries of the space frontier benefits the country's innovation, culture and economy, said renowned astronomer Neil deGrasse Tyson.

Tyson, the director of the Hayden Planetarium in New York and an outspoken space advocate, delivered the opening address this morning (April 17 [2012]) here at the 28th National Space Symposium.

"Space is a $300 billion industry worldwide," Tyson said. "NASA is a tiny percent of that. [But] that little bit is what inspires dreams."

He spoke about how space has influenced culture—ranging from how the fins on early rockets inspired fins on automobiles in the 1950s, to how the Apollo 8 mission's iconic picture taken in 1968 of Earth rising above the horizon of the moon led to a greater appreciation for our planet and the need to protect it. Yet, many people outside the space community see it as a special interest group, Tyson said.

"Innovation drives economy," he said. "It's especially been true since the Industrial Revolution." . . .

Furthermore, this type of capability can be used for a myriad of purposes, including military endeavors, science missions, commercial expeditions and space tourism.

Denise Chow,
"Boosting NASA's Budget Will Help Fix Economy:
Neil deGrasse Tyson," Space.com, April 17, 2012.

Enjoy sleeping on that memory foam mattress? Developed from technology designed to improve crash protection for airplane passengers. Glad you didn't have to wear those hideous chain-link dental braces? The transparent material in invisible braces was developed for military tracking purposes. Enjoy jogging with your athletic shoes? Those insoles derived from technology in moon boots designed for shock absorption. Wear glasses? They're scratch resistant thanks to synthetic diamond coatings developed for aerospace systems.

The list goes on: high-capacity batteries, advances in the aerodynamics of vehicles, UV [ultraviolet] filters for glasses, cloud technology, satellite television, Google Earth imagery, breast cancer detection . . . NASA has had a hand in all of these things—and more.

The fact is that NASA has filed thousands of patents with the U.S. government, and technology either spun off from NASA or directly developed by the program is all around us. Some of the greatest discoveries and inventions in human history were not a result of direct development, but rather were incidental to the development of *other* technologies and ideas. Funding a space program isn't just funding the construction of spaceships—it's funding *invention* itself.

But maybe you didn't need to be reminded of the tangible examples of the application of NASA science to our daily lives. Maybe you were already sold on the idea of space exploration, because you can appreciate the far-reaching benefits that may not be obvious to everyone.

By funding a space program, we inspire the next generation to enter the fields of science and engineering. We show the world that we are a progressive, forward-thinking people seeking the betterment of the human race. We further our understanding of the universe we inhabit. We continue the proud human tradition of exploration, the eternal zeitgeist fueled by unbridled ambition that has pushed our civilization to achieve things once thought impossible. We pave a path among the stars for the eventual expansion of humanity into a universe whose mysteries we will conquer, one eureka at a time.

So why should we fund the space program? Ultimately, it all boils down to one reason: For Science.

"The tremendous waste of taxpayer money by NASA to maintain under-utilized facilities, or ones no longer used at all, is staggering."

NASA and the Federal Government Waste Taxpayer Money

Douglas Cobb

Douglas Cobb is a writer for Guardian Liberty Voice. In the following viewpoint, Cobb argues that the National Aeronautics and Space Administration (NASA) wastes an extraordinary amount of taxpayer money and should be denied funding by Congress. He claims that in 2011 alone, NASA spent millions of taxpayer dollars to maintain more than thirty underutilized facilities. Unless NASA's disused facilities can be leased to other companies, Cobb believes, they should be closed so the government stops wasting money on them.

As you read, consider the following questions:

1. What does Cobb say is one of the most famous examples of expensive NASA waste for which American citizens are still paying taxes?

2. What were Congress's three shifting interests in NASA funding that Cobb says have wasted money?

3. Which two space companies competed to lease NASA's Launch Pad 39A?

NASA [National Aeronautics and Space Administration] has made many significant contributions to the world's knowledge of space and Earth. For the amount of money which the U.S. government allocates it in yearly budgets, NASA has paid back society in inventions alone, such as memory foam, anticorrosion coating, ArterioVision [technology that helps detect and treat heart disease and strokes], cochlear implants, scratch-resistant eyeglass lenses, and many others. Yet, in 2011 alone, NASA spent $43 million in taxpayers' money to maintain more than 33 underutilized infrastructure facilities, according to an audit by the office of the inspector general. Is Congress more at fault for this waste of taxpayer money, or is NASA?

The structures include launch infrastructures, thermal vacuum chambers, and wind tunnels. NASA is either underutilizing these structures, or is not using them at all, but they continue to be a drain on the pocketbooks of American taxpayers.

Perhaps one of the most famous and expensive of these examples to maintain is one that NASA began constructing several years ago, when it had plans for making a return trip to the moon.

Stennis Space Center in Mississippi was meant to be the facility which would store needed testing equipment for rockets. NASA got funding to build a rocket test stand there, one that would cost $350 million to construct, as part of the Constellation program.

In 2010, President [Barack] Obama cancelled the program when it was a third of the way to go from completion.

Congress voted for the project to be finished, despite Obama's cancellation of it. They allocated another $57 million to NASA for this purpose. Though the test stand will be finished this month [in September 2013], there is currently not a use for it. Still, the cost of maintaining it, alone, for taxpayers will amount to $900,000 annually.

The Real Fault

These problems are, generally speaking, less the fault of poor planning by NASA as compared to the fault of Congress and ever changing presidential administrations.

For example, NASA's main goals in the area of human space exploration just in the past six years have changed three times, at least. First, the focus and congressional funding was directed to the space shuttle program; then, that changed to a focus on the Constellation program. Now, Congress has directed NASA to work on a "Space Launch System" with the goal of a manned mission to Mars sometime in the 2030s.

According to NASA inspector general Paul Martin, addressing lawmakers, the frequent shifts in what is considered to be the national space policy "have increased the difficulty of determining which facilities NASA needs."

Also, there appears to be no clear time limit on how long obsolete structures must be kept and maintained. Over 80 percent of the NASA facilities are over 40 years old, and have worn out their original usage. What's more, in 2012, the backlog's cost, alone, of the "deferred maintenance projects" of NASA was estimated to be $2.3 billion.

Even when NASA has attempted to turn an obsolete piece of its infrastructure into a moneymaker, sometimes the intervention of Congress has slowed down these efforts.

For example, NASA would like to lease the launch pad it used to support the shuttle and Apollo programs at the Kennedy Space Center in Florida. The cost for NASA to maintain it each year is $1.2 million. Unless someone is found who will use the launch pad, it will be demolished.

The structure is called Launch Pad 39A. . . .

NASA officials were close to leasing the pad to SpaceX, an aerospace company that was the first to fly cargo to the International Space Station, until another company, Blue Origin, submitted a competing bid to take over pad 39A and operate it as a multiuser facility.

Blue Origin has filed a protest which will likely delay any action on a potential lease to occur until maybe December 12, 2013.

The battle's been taken to the U.S. Congress, where various lawmakers with various vested interests want the bid to go to SpaceX while others would like to see it go to Blue Origin, so that multiple users could use the launch pad.

GOP [Grand Old Party, nickname for the Republican Party] Rep. Bill Posey of Florida sums up the situation, saying that billions of dollars have been wasted. That's because of "the parochial interests of different members trying to micromanage what NASA does."

The tremendous waste of taxpayer money by NASA to maintain underutilized facilities, or ones no longer used at all, is staggering. Congress and whichever president happens to be in office are really more at fault than NASA, but the national space agency is often the one who gets the blame for this waste of money.

> *"The rubric of personal spaceflight seems to envisage a future of transport—a personalised, individualistic form of transport for those who can afford it."*

Space Tourism Needs an 'Orbital Megabus' to Truly Lift Off

Mark Johnson

Mark Johnson is a doctoral candidate in sociology at the University of York in the United Kingdom. In the following viewpoint, Johnson argues that space tourism is an emerging industry of the future. This will allow citizens to enjoy outer space as a journey rather than a destination. However, this development, he claims, may only ever be available for the wealthy and never for the mass public.

As you read, consider the following questions:

1. How does Johnson compare future space tourism to the civil aviation model of today?

2. What does Johnson say are some of the purposes of citizen space exploration?

3. What does Johnson say would be some risks and unpleasant aspects of space tourism?

Britain has joined the race to become a leading hub of commercial spaceflight, announcing eight potential sites for a potential "spaceport" within the UK.

There are numerous questions surrounding this nascent form of tourism. Many focus on the technology in place to deliver it, the legislation that is necessary to safeguard it and, most recently, the pragmatic questions of where spaceports should be placed. But often overlooked is the issue of exactly what the industry will look like and who it will target, which isn't as clear-cut as you might assume. The plan is to start space-plane operations by 2018, so who can we expect to be taking part in this new frontier of the travel industry?

"Space tourism" is a catchall term that encompasses three different ideas of what the industry could look like. These are: "space tourism", "personal spaceflight" and "citizen space exploration".

Space Tourism

As well as being used to encompass all three strands, "space tourism" can also be used in a more specific sense. In its purest form, it puts forward a mass-market future that emphasises the sightseeing potential of trips into space. Although Virgin Galactic may aspire to this goal, they have for now focused on trips for the very wealthy, not the expansion of the market.

A true space tourism model would be comparable to the civil aviation that exists today: a significant number of passengers on one flight and eventually the possibility of a Megabusequivalent for space travel. In this sense it is a future of commercialisation, albeit one subtly different to existing forms of transit.

Personal Spaceflight

"Personal spaceflight" refers to the type of journeys currently being offered by companies like Virgin Galactic. They will take a party of up to six passengers (this number may increase in the future) for private trips into space.

This form of commercial space travel has a strongly individualistic tone to it. As the terminology implies, a certain form of wealth or lifestyle akin to the assumptions you might make about "personal trainers" or "personal assistants" accompany it. And, indeed, personal spaceflight is only open to the wealthiest of individuals, with flights currently costing anything from US$95,000 to $250,000, depending how long and personal a journey you wish to take.

What, therefore, does personal spaceflight seek to bring to the lives of those with the lifestyle and wealth that can afford these kinds of personal service? The rubric of personal spaceflight seems to envisage a future of transport—a personalised, individualistic form of transport for those who can afford it that will allow rapid travel around the world, and also leisure activities unavailable to the majority of the populace. This is in part tourism, but the tourism and leisure aspects are, in this conception, a subset of the development of a new form of transport.

Citizen Space Exploration

Citizen space exploration has two combined facets. The first is built around an idea of democratising space—instead of space only being accessible to just astronauts and those of significant wealth, it's about opening space up to a range of citizens. In addition, the focus is also on widening the range of those who can access space, irrespective of whether it is for touristic purposes or not—and widening the number of reasons people may choose to go to space, such as participation in "citizen science" and general educational purposes.

One way of doing this is through combining citizen science and citizen space exploration. However, for this model to be funded it would either require significant injection of funds from external sources, or an increase in the flights taking place (and a reduction in the price) to the point that the industry becomes self-sustaining despite a far lower cost per passenger.

The Journey, Not the Destination

Regardless of the model, space tourism generally imagines a form of tourism where the objective of the travel is the travel itself—to go into space, look down at Earth in orbit, experience weightlessness—rather than reaching a distinct destination. This brings the emphasis onto the travel experience itself, which comes with a number of risks (such as bone density loss) and a number of unpleasant aspects (such as G-force and nausea).

While many may not enjoy flying on domestic flights, the discomfort is endured in order to reach the final destination. By contrast, the final destination in a space tourism trip includes some of the downsides of the initial launch. In this sense, while it may still be the preserve of the wealthy, it can hardly be considered a form of luxury travel—more an extreme sport. Equally, it also entails a change in the perception of what a holiday or a tourist experience is, with the travel and the destination becoming one.

It remains to be seen what model of space tourism emerges in the long run, how significant the market turns out to be and the extent to which space tourism gains public acceptance or availability beyond the realms of the very wealthy. There is, as yet, little evidence of how much public demand there is for space tourism—or whether or not people would want to make the journey more than once (versus yearly holidays for example). The next few years will show us a lot about how the industry will develop, but for the time being—watch this space.

> *"Virgin Galactic is building the world's most expensive roller coaster, the aerospace version of Beluga caviar."*

Space Tourism Is Not Worth the Human Risk

Adam Rogers

Adam Rogers is a writer for Wired.com. In the following viewpoint, Rogers contends that space tourism is an exciting prospect but should not be developed at the cost of human lives. Rather, such technology should be used for helping humanity live elsewhere when Earth becomes uninhabitable. Space exploration for any other reason, Rogers believes, is frivolous.

As you read, consider the following questions:

1. What does Rogers say was the real purpose of the Apollo space program?

2. What distinction does Rogers make between supporters of space tourism and the historical explorers of the past?

3. How does Rogers both praise and criticize Virgin Galactic for its activities?

A brave test pilot [Michael Alsbury] is dead and another one [Peter Siebold] critically injured—in the service of a millionaire boondoggle thrill ride.

To be clear: I like spaceships. A lot. I went to the first landing of the space shuttle post-*Challenger* disaster. I went to the Mojave for the first test flight of SpaceShipOne, nominally to cover it but really just to gaze in wonder. I root for SpaceX, and felt real disappointment at Orbital Sciences' Antares disaster this week [on October 28, 2014, when the Antares rocket exploded during liftoff for a mission to deliver cargo to the International Space Station].

But in the wake of this tragedy out at Mojave—not even the first time a SpaceShipTwo test has killed someone—we're going to hear a lot about exploration, about pioneers and frontiers. People are going to talk about Giant Leaps for Mankind and Boldly Going Where No One Has Gone Before. And we should call bullshit on that.

SpaceShipTwo—at least, the version that has the Virgin Galactic livery painted on its tail—is not a Federation [referring to *Star Trek*'s "United Federation of Planets"] starship. It's not a vehicle for the exploration of frontiers. This would be true even if Virgin Galactic did more than barely brush up against the bottom of space. Virgin Galactic is building the world's most expensive roller coaster, the aerospace version of Beluga caviar. It's a thing for rich people to do: pay $250,000 to not feel the weight of the world.

People get rich; they spend money. Sometimes it's vulgar, but it's the system we all seem to accept. When it costs the lives of the workers building that system, we should stop accepting it.

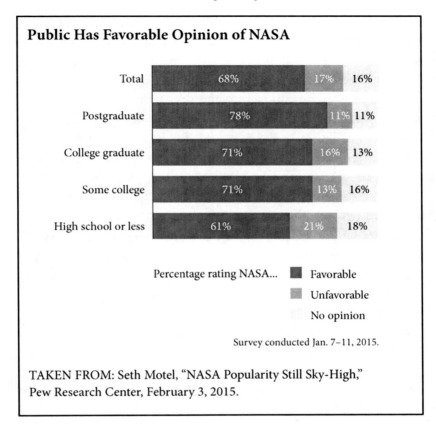

Public Has Favorable Opinion of NASA

	Favorable	Unfavorable	No opinion
Total	68%	17%	16%
Postgraduate	78%	11%	11%
College graduate	71%	16%	13%
Some college	71%	13%	16%
High school or less	61%	21%	18%

Percentage rating NASA... ■ Favorable ▨ Unfavorable No opinion

Survey conducted Jan. 7–11, 2015.

TAKEN FROM: Seth Motel, "NASA Popularity Still Sky-High," Pew Research Center, February 3, 2015.

Glorious Journeys

Governments and businesses have always positioned space travel as a glorious journey. But that is a misdirect. It is branding. The Apollo program was the most technologically sophisticated propaganda front of the Cold War [nonviolent post–World War II conflict between the United States and the Soviet Union], a battle among superpowers for scientific bragging rights. Don't get mad—that truth doesn't diminish the brilliance of the achievement. It doesn't mean that the engineers weren't geniuses or the astronauts weren't brave or skilled. But it does make problematic, at least a little, the idea that those astronauts were explorers opening up a new frontier.

Historically, frontiers have always been dicey. What the average Western European thought of as a frontier in the 1600s was someone else's land. And the reasons for going toward frontiers have always been complicated by economics. Was [Christopher] Columbus brave? Sure, probably. But he was also looking for a trade route. Were the conquistadores intrepid? Yeah. But they were looking for gold and land. Do human beings have a drive to push past horizons, over mountains, into the unknown? Manifestly. But we always balance that drive and desire with its potential outcomes. We go when there's something there.

That's why a space program designed to get humanity off our native planet makes sense—but only a specific kind. Eventually this planet is going to be unlivable, either because of something we humans do to it or something natural. Asteroids have wiped Earth clean before, and presumably they'll do it again. It'd be good to not be here when it happens. Elon Musk has made that part of his explicit rationale for SpaceX, his rocket company. Going to space is wondrous, difficult, and a testament to the human spirit. It's also utterly, cynically practical. That's being a pioneer.

And it's a mistake to lump that kind of endeavor with Virgin Galactic. Exploration and evacuation are not its value proposition. The technology SpaceShipTwo employs is not, except perhaps in its broadest description, designed to take humanity off-world. It's genius engineering, but it isn't about exploring anything except the legitimately difficult challenge of a rocket plane that can go very, very high. It is about making space tourism into a viable business.

Testing new aircraft takes a level of courage and ability beyond most humans. The pilots who work out the kinks in military fighters and giant transport planes are keeping their various countries safe (let's agree to believe) or helping further the global economy. And it doesn't take any less bravery or skill to test the planes Virgin Galactic wants to fly. Those engineers and those pilots are at the peak of human achievement. What they're doing is amazing. Why Virgin is doing it is not.

When various corporate representatives eulogize those two pilots as pioneers who were helping to cross the Final Frontier [that is, space], that should make you angry. That pilot died not for space but for a luxury service provider. His death doesn't get us closer to Mars; it keeps rich people further away from weightlessness and a beautiful view.

Periodical and Internet Sources Bibliography

The following articles have been selected to supplement the diverse views presented in this chapter.

Elise Ackerman	"Seven Sci-Fi Scenarios for Interstellar Space Travel That Could Happen in This Century," *Forbes*, September 29, 2013.
Jonathan Amos	"Obama Seeks to Raise NASA Funding," BBC News, February 3, 2015.
Matt Asay	"Why Elon Musk's SpaceX Is Even Cooler than Tesla," *Tech Republic*, June 22, 2015.
Associated Press	"Virgin Galactic Gets Back on Track Toward Space Tourism," *Boston Herald*, February 3, 2015.
Christian Davenport	"Richard Branson's Virgin Galactic Scores Commercial Satellite Launch Order, and It's a Big One," *Washington Post*, June 25, 2015.
Julian Hattem	"Battle Brewing over NASA Funding," *The Hill*, March 14, 2015.
Rafi Letzter	"Interstellar Travel Won't Look Anything Like the Movie," *Popular Science*, October 28, 2014.
Gbenga Oduntan	"Is Space Tourism Travelling Faster than Space Law?," The Conversation, June 23, 2015.
Phil Plait	"To Mars," *Slate*, April 16, 2015.
Michael Potter	"A Grand National Space Strategy Could Save NASA," Space.com, June 9, 2015.
Marcia S. Smith	"Earth Science Takes Hit in Proposed House NASA Authorization Bill," SpacePolicyOnline .com, April 26, 2015.

OPPOSING
VIEWPOINTS®
SERIES

CHAPTER 2

Where in Space Should Humans Explore?

Chapter Preface

As technology to advance space exploration becomes more sophisticated in the twenty-first century, the scientific community periodically raises the topic of space colonization. Proponents of the endeavor claim that Earth is not a permanently sustainable home for humans, as climate change and the progressive depletion of natural resources will eventually make the planet uninhabitable. The alternative proposed by this faction of people is to invest more heavily in the colonization of other suitable worlds in nearby space or worlds that can be made suitable. The three most viable new homes for the human race, scientists argue, are Mars, Venus, and the moon. While colonization supporters describe their plans and suggestions for such efforts, their opponents counter with warnings about the massive costs and extreme dangers of leaving Earth to live on other celestial bodies. This debate briefly played out on the American stage when it arose during the 2012 presidential election.

During a Republican Party debate held in Florida in January of that year, candidate Newt Gingrich vowed that by the end of his second term as president, the year 2020, he would have created an American colony on the moon. He promised further that the base could apply to become the fifty-first US state once thirteen thousand Americans were living there. This announcement was part of a pattern of speeches Gingrich delivered during the election season; he consistently spoke of his desire to reinvigorate Florida's Space Coast and encourage young people to study science and technology to make the United States more competitive globally.

Gingrich was harshly criticized for his proposal, however, with fellow Republican presidential candidates Mitt Romney and Rick Santorum saying during the debate that promising Americans a moon colony was grandiose, irresponsible, and an extraordinary waste of money that could be put to greater use on America's existing problems. Gingrich's plan continued to be attacked, refuted, and mocked in the following weeks. Gingrich, meanwhile, maintained that lofty ideas such as his were necessary to excite young Americans about the future of their country, just as President John F. Kennedy's 1961 vow to put Americans on the moon by 1969 had generated widespread interest in space exploration.

The same debate has continued among scientists into the mid-2010s, even as the conversation has expanded to encompass the colonization of the planets Mars and Venus. Supporters of the ventures enthusiastically detail their plans for establishing and sustaining human settlements on these bodies, with suggestions ranging from plant greenhouses for the creation of oxygen on Mars to massive floating cities in blimps high above the surface of Venus. As in the past, adversaries of these plans continually cite their extravagant costs and the enormous risks to human life. While colonization supporters admit to these great challenges, they still claim that no other options ultimately exist for the long-term survival of humanity.

The following chapter presents viewpoints related to the areas of the solar system believed to hold the most promise for the future of human beings beyond Earth. Subjects covered include the colonization of Mars, the moon, and Venus.

"Spreading out to one of our next-door neighbours, such as the moon or Mars, is becoming a truly feasible option."

Humans Should Colonize Mars

Louisa Preston

Louisa Preston is an astrobiologist and a TED Fellow at the Open University. In the following viewpoint, Preston argues that colonizing Mars will soon become a possible endeavor for humans, especially with the introduction of plant life to the planet. Plants on Mars would provide people with oxygen while thriving in the carbon dioxide–rich atmosphere, she claims. Preston believes all of this will be necessary as Earth becomes increasingly inhospitable to human life with the passage of time.

As you read, consider the following questions:

1. How large is Earth's population estimated to grow by 2050?

2. What does Preston say are the dangers of Mars, despite its hospitable environment compared to other planets?

3. What does Preston say would be the relationship between plants and different levels of gravity in space?

Imagine Earth in the future. Do you think we'll have flying cars, floating cities or colonies deep under the ocean? Science fiction often paints an almost magical vision of the future. But what if we think more realistically?

By 2050 the UN [United Nations] predicts that Earth's human population will have grown from 7.096 billion to between 8.3 and 10.9 billion. It will probably only continue to grow. In this version of the future, many questions will surround the sustainability of world populations, the growing pressures on the environment, global food supplies, and energy resources. Will Earth be able to sustain us? With the answer to this question unknown, humanity needs to start planning to leave the safety net of Earth and look to the stars. Ok, *Star Trek*–style exploration may be a bit too far into the future, but spreading out to one of our next-door neighbours, such as the moon or Mars, is becoming a truly feasible option.

Life on Mars

We have already started to pick out our Martian prime real estate through Curiosity [a National Aeronautics and Space Administration (NASA) rover] and numerous orbiter and rover missions. Next month [August 2013] marks the one-year anniversary of NASA's latest toy, the Mars Science Laboratory, better known as the Curiosity rover, landing on Mars. Although the moon is nearer, making access and communications easier, it is Mars that seems to have captured our imagination for a future human outpost. Much of this is inspired by evidence that it might have once been a world similar to Earth.

Mars today, despite its subzero temperatures (on average -63°C), thin non-breathable CO_2-rich atmosphere, high UV [ultraviolet]-radiation and savage global dust storms, actually has the most clement environment in the solar system after Earth. It also has the potential to contain habitable environments for life. To survive, terrestrial-type life needs an environment with a source of liquid water, organic molecules, and a source of energy.

One of the biggest problems we need to solve to enable humans to live on Mars is space agriculture. How can we expect to survive indefinitely on Mars without growing our own food, and producing our own water and oxygen? It costs $80,000 to ship four litres of water to the moon! Just imagine the cost, let alone the logistics, of shipping water and food to Mars.

The first 'Martians' will therefore be two kinds—plants and humans—who are actually ideal companions. Humans consume oxygen and release carbon dioxide. Plants return the favour by consuming carbon dioxide and releasing oxygen. Humans can use edible parts of plants for nourishment, while human waste and inedible plant matter can (after being broken down by microbes in tanks called bioreactors) provide nutrients for plant growth. Plants such as asparagus, potatoes and marigolds have already been shown to grow in Mars-like soils, and seeds of radish, alfalfa, and mung bean have been observed to sprout in a CO_2-rich atmosphere like that on Mars. Gardens are, in my opinion at least, the key to settling on Mars as they could help to recycle nutrients, provide drinking water and use the carbon from the toxic Martian atmosphere to produce oxygen through photosynthesis for humans to breathe. Gardens could even, in the long term, provide building materials such as wood and bamboo, and would improve the morale and well-being of the crew.

Overcoming Challenges

Plants on Mars would have to overcome the challenges that come with the planet having 38% of the gravity on Earth, a

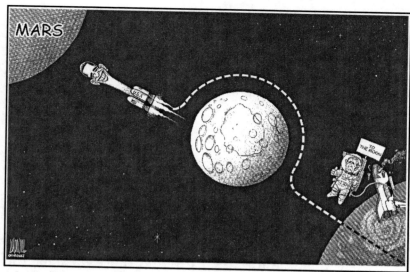

© Luojie, "Obama's New Space Exploration," Cagle Post, April 20, 2010.

low-pressure atmosphere, subzero temperatures, a lack of readily available liquid water and too much solar UV radiation. Any garden would therefore not be able to live freely on the surface but inside a greenhouse, commonly depicted as a geodesic dome, which would create a stable and comfortable environment for plant growth using all the natural resources Mars has to offer. There'll be nothing to compensate for the reduced gravity on Mars. However, experiments on the International Space Station [ISS] have shown that gravity doesn't play as great a role in plant growth as we once believed. It was always thought that the growth direction and patterns of roots were generated through a combination of a touch response between the root tip and whatever it is running into (a rock, a hard surface, etc.) and the force of gravity. Experiments on the ISS have shown that *Arabidopsis*—a mustard-like plant—grows the same on Earth as in orbit. This research indicates that plants will be able to grow on Mars or the moon as well as on Earth (at least as far as gravity is concerned).

But research into space gardening won't just help future Martians. With ongoing climate change and increasing environmental problems here on Earth, studies into the logistics and physics of growing plants on the unfriendly surface of Mars, and the moon, could help people develop strategies to grow food in areas on Earth which are not currently suitable for food production due to similarly hostile climates.

In five billion years, our sun will start to die, expanding as it enters its red giant phase. It will engulf Venus, and, even if it doesn't swell enough to reach Earth, it will still boil off the oceans and heat the surface to temperatures that even the hardiest life-forms couldn't survive. I hope that long before any of these natural or man-made terrestrial problems comes to pass, we will choose to leave Earth and move to Mars, the moon or beyond, simply because we want to. When we do, we'll have to take our trowels with us.

"We don't know if colonists living for extended periods of time in the 1/6 gravity of the moon will suffer . . . physiological problems."

Should We Colonize the Moon? And How Much Would It Cost?

Noah Davis

Noah Davis is a writer for Pacific Standard. *Nadine G. Barlow is a professor and an associate chair in the physics and astronomy department at Northern Arizona University. In the following viewpoint, Barlow, as interviewed by Davis, argues that establishing moon colonies is a good idea but would prove extremely difficult and expensive. People can mine the moon's natural resources, Barlow claims, as well as establish radio observatories. The obstacles of safety and expense, however, would need to be overcome first.*

As you read, consider the following questions:

1. What hazards does Barlow say moon colonists would encounter that are not experienced in near-Earth orbit?

2. How does Barlow say the gravity of a moon colony would affect future space missions?

3. What methods does Barlow suggest for reducing the costs of colonizing the moon?

Russia, according to one report, is planning to colonize the moon by 2030. While this news may be speculative, alarmist, or possibly not even based in reality, we still wanted to know if moon colonization in 16 years is even possible. So we asked Dr. Nadine G. Barlow, a professor and associate chair in the physics and astronomy department at Northern Arizona University, for some answers. Watch out for the abrasive lunar dust, people.

Is it reasonable to expect that Russia could colonize the moon by 2030? What technology needs to be designed/developed before something like that can occur?

The year 2030 is only 16 years away, so this goal seems rather optimistic to me, especially considering that the last time the country sent a mission to the moon was in 1976 with the Soviet robotic Luna 24 mission. Russia has been working on plans to return to the moon for about the last 15 years and has a series of robotic missions planned beginning in 2016. However, the 2016 launch has slipped several times since its initially planned launch in 2012 due to funding issues. Roscosmos (the Russian Federal Space Agency) needs a dramatic influx of funding from the government and/or private sources to return the country to lunar exploration. Russia has considerable experience in terms of keeping cosmonauts alive in orbiting space stations and can apply that technological knowledge to the development of the infrastructure needed for humans to colonize the moon. However, there are a number of issues which colonies on the moon will encounter which are not experienced in near-Earth orbit, such as 14 Earth days of continuous daylight followed by 14 Earth days of night, abrasive lunar dust, which will damage machinery and which is difficult to clean off, etc. Russia never landed humans on the moon, and it has been decades since its last successful robotic landing on another world, so the country will need to have a huge influx of money and talent in order to reach their goal of establishing colonies on the moon by 2030.

Any ballpark on how expensive it would be to do so?

The cost depends on how many people you would send to colonize the moon and how many shipments of supplies and materials would be necessary to establish the colony. A typical cost to send humans and materials from Earth to the moon is about $50,000 per pound. The result, even if lunar resources are used to construct the habitat, usually has a lower estimate of several tens of billions of dollars to establish a colony on the moon.

What are the benefits of colonizing the moon?

Colonies on the moon present several advantages. The moon has 1/6 the gravitational pull of Earth, so it could become a cheaper spaceport from which to launch missions to other parts of our solar system. It has some natural resources, which could be mined, such as regions with high titanium concentrations and implanted helium from the sun, which could be used for developing energy from fusion. The moon has not undergone as much volcanic and tectonic processing as Earth, so it still retains information from the early history of the solar system, which has been lost here on our home planet—it therefore can help us better understand the origin and early history of our own planet. Astronomers look to the moon as a location for future optical and radio observatories, away from the light pollution and radio noise of Earth. And of course it would literally be an out-of-this-world tourist destination if the cost of getting there could be reduced to a value that people could afford.

Are there unintended consequences we might not be considering if we colonize the moon?

Living on the Moon May Be Impossible

The US space agency NASA [National Aeronautics and Space Administration] sells dreams. There's nothing wrong with that. . . . The problem with dreams is that sooner or later you must wake up.

To judge from an article on lunar bases on NASA's website, it's reluctant to do that. "When multiple spacecraft all found unequivocal evidence for water on the moon it was a boon to possible future lunar bases, acting as a potential source of drinking water and fuel," the article says. It explains that the atomic components of water—hydrogen and oxygen—on the lunar surface move toward the poles, "where [water] accumulates in the cold traps of the permanently shadowed regions." Since it was first proposed several years ago, this idea that the polar craters, particularly the so-called Shackleton crater at the south pole, are lined with ancient ice has inspired many hyperbolic newspaper stories about colonising the moon. But it's looking ever less likely that it is true.

A new paper in the journal *Geophysical Research Letters* drives another nail into the coffin of lunar living. It suggests that what was at first taken to be bright, reflective ice in the Shackleton crater is in fact more likely to be white rock. . . .

Given the history so far, it would be unwise to imagine that this is the last we will hear of water on the moon. But it would be un-wiser still to start planning to build a colony up there.

Philip Ball,
"Why We Might Not Be Able to Live on the Moon,"
BBC, September 6, 2013.

There are several concerns about human activities on the moon. The lunar day is about 29 Earth days long, which means most places on the lunar surface receive about two weeks of daylight followed by two weeks of night. This places strong constraints on possible energy sources (power by solar energy would not work without development of some very effective energy storage technologies) and will affect human circadian rhythms to a greater extent than we see even with shift workers here on Earth. The Apollo missions to the moon between 1969 and 1972 showed that the lunar dust is very abrasive, sticks to everything, and may be toxic to humans—machinery is likely to need constant maintenance and techniques will need to be developed to keep the astronauts from bringing dust into the habitats on their spacesuits after surface activities. Growing crops on the moon will present its own challenges between the long day/night cycles and the need to add nutrients/bacteria to the lunar soil. Surface activities will kick up dust from the surface, enhancing the thin veneer of particles that make up the lunar atmosphere and transporting the dust over larger distances to cause even more damage to machinery. The moon's atmosphere is so thin that it provides no protection from micrometeorite bombardment or radiation—both of these issues will need to be addressed in habitat design and maintenance. Finally we know that astronauts living for extended periods of time in the microgravity environment of orbiting space stations often suffer physiological issues, particularly upon return to Earth. We don't know if colonists living for extended periods of time in the 1/6 gravity of the moon will suffer similar physiological problems. And of course there is always the question of how humans will react psychologically to life in a confined habitat in such an alien environment.

Does "colonizing the moon" make sense as a goal? It's a nice talking point, but are there other/better space exploration-related priorities that would make more sense?

There are a number of people who argue that we should bypass the moon in favor of "more interesting" places for human colonization, such as Mars. However, colonizing the moon does have some strong arguments in its favor. The moon is relatively close to Earth—it only takes a few days to travel between Earth and the moon rather than months to years to travel to Mars. The moon therefore is a good location to try out the technologies needed for colonization of other worlds. After all, the early American settlers did not make a quick dash from the East Coast to the West Coast—they started out the westward expansion by settling areas closer to "home" and gradually moving further away. We already have seen that there are often unexpected problems when developing completely enclosed habitats—for example, the concrete used to build the Biosphere 2 facility near Tucson, Arizona, was found to absorb more oxygen than expected, resulting in problems for the humans, animals, and plants during the "closed missions" in 1991 to 1994. The ease of traveling between Earth and the moon makes it an excellent place to test out new designs and technologies and resolve any issues that arise before embarking on colonization plans for more distant worlds.

How much does international politics play a role in something like this? There are a number of countries that have expressed similar goals with regard to colonization. Are we about to enter a new era of the Space Race?

As noted above, the cost of colonizing other worlds will be extremely expensive and thus would take an incredible amount of a single country's overall budget. Therefore, human exploration and colonization of other worlds will likely become an international effort with the cost spread across several countries rather than a Space Race to beat others to the lunar surface. Influx of funds from private companies could help offset some of the cost incurred by a particular nation, but private companies typically want some return benefit from their investment so they may not be involved in the early efforts of establishing the bases. There are several countries expressing interest in colonizing our natural satellite and probably eventually many of these plans will merge to result in truly international colonies. But the plans by multiple countries to colonize the moon raise another big issue of whether these countries can stake claims to the regions of the moon. The Outer Space Treaty of 1967 states that no government can lay claim to any celestial body since these objects are considered a common heritage of mankind. However, not all countries currently interested in lunar colonization are signatories to this treaty, and the treaty only applies to governments, not private companies. So there are a number of legal questions that also need to be resolved by the international community before colonization of the moon can become reality.

"Exploration and discovery are not luxuries that we can do once we have fixed the rest of our problems. They are simply part of our humanity."

Humans Should Resume Exploring the Moon and Outer Space

Joseph Mascaro

Joseph Mascaro is a postdoctoral associate in the Department of Global Ecology at the Carnegie Institution for Science. In the following viewpoint, Mascaro argues that establishing a moon colony would not be a wasteful venture but rather would encourage engineering and manufacturing as the industries that will help humanity reach its greatest potential. If people pursue their interests in space, Mascaro believes, the next generation will become just as enthralled by such endeavors.

As you read, consider the following questions:

1. What existential threats does Mascaro say people rightly attempt to confront?

2. What three opportunities does Mascaro say have recently been created for space exploration?

3. What criticism of the Apollo space program does Mascaro say is irrelevant?

I can trace my career in science to many childhood inspirations, but the most haunting is a memory of my mother—a schoolteacher—staring blankly at the television as [the space shuttle] *Challenger*'s solid rocket boosters jetted away from the disintegrating orbiter [on January 28, 1986]. Scientists had seemed cartoonish to me before that day, but suddenly they were soldiers: righteous and fearless, and my mother was just like them. I have been in complete awe of human spaceflight ever since.

That's why I was heartened last month [January 2012] when [former Speaker of the House of Representatives and 2012 presidential candidate] Newt Gingrich announced he was going to give a major address on Florida's Space Coast. The announcement might have looked like a pander to Florida primary voters disillusioned by President [Barack] Obama's tepid vision for space exploration, but, in fact, Gingrich has expressed a sustained interest in human spaceflight throughout his career. He has schemed over dinner with rocket man and spaceflight promoter Robert Zubrin (author of *The Case for Mars*) and coauthored an op-ed two years ago praising the president for increasing funding for commercial spaceflight.

So, I checked my Democratic Party registration at the door and tuned in.

But my hopes came, well, crashing back to Earth. Trying to invoke JFK [John F. Kennedy], Gingrich fell flat. His proposed lunar colony borrowed 1960s lingo, but failed to convey the thirst or collective determination that permeated 1960s American families. As with President George W. Bush's Constellation program, the goal of a lunar settlement seemed like a rehash of our past exploits. Worse still, his promise of establishing the colony by the end of his "second term" and his suggestion that it would be the 51st state buried the substance of what he said under reels of late-night comedy.

At a debate the next night, his opponents pounced, dismantling the idea of increasing spending on human spaceflight in a country drowning in debt. [Presidential candidate Rick] Santorum said the moon can wait. [Presidential candidate Mitt] Romney said he would fire anyone who proposed such an idea, and this time Romney's tone-deaf obsession with canning people seemed to land cleanly, because the audience agreed.

Part of Humanity

Like climate change deniers' notion that Earth is too big to possibly be altered by humans, human spaceflight suffers from a common but misguided gut reaction, which goes something like this: "We have plenty of problems right here on Earth."

This is a false premise. Exploration and discovery are not luxuries that we can do once we have fixed the rest of our problems. They are simply part of our humanity. In national discourse we rightly focus on existential threats—Iran, debt, climate change—but to thrive, we must also consider existential opportunities. The opportunity for exploration is real. Private companies like SpaceX [American aerospace company] are bringing rocket costs down, hints of water on the surface of Mars are captivating scientists, and China's aggressive human spaceflight planning is stirring congressional inquiry.

Our guts tell us that human spaceflight will distract us from tackling debt or battling terrorism, but this is all wrong. Real missions with real people, strapped in tuna cans for six months and sending tweets from the Martian surface, will not distract us from anything. It will awaken the sleepwalking students in our broken education system. It will steer our talents where we need them most: engineering, energy, and manufac-

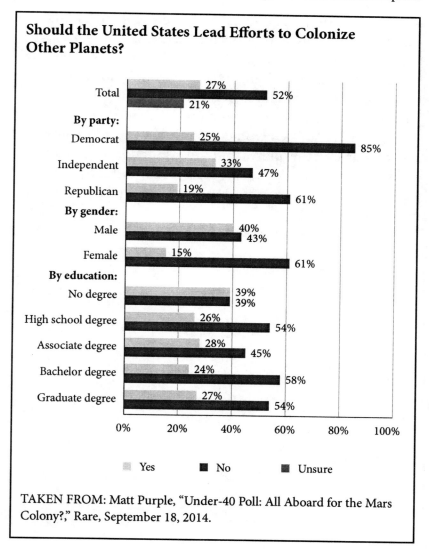

Should the United States Lead Efforts to Colonize Other Planets?

Total
  27%
  52%
  21%

By party:

Democrat
  25%
  85%

Independent
  33%
  47%

Republican
  19%
  61%

By gender:

Male
  40%
  43%

Female
  15%
  61%

By education:

No degree
  39%
  39%

High school degree
  26%
  54%

Associate degree
  28%
  45%

Bachelor degree
  24%
  58%

Graduate degree
  27%
  54%

0%   20%   40%   60%   80%   100%

Yes   ■ No   ■ Unsure

TAKEN FROM: Matt Purple, "Under-40 Poll: All Aboard for the Mars Colony?," *Rare*, September 18, 2014.

turing. This is the right time to have a sustained national discussion, and Gingrich should be applauded for trying to start one, likely knowing his opponents would roll their eyes.

Gingrich was a child of Apollo [one of the National Aeronautics and Space Administration's human spaceflight programs], and so was Christa McAuliffe—the teacher that perished aboard *Challenger* 26 years ago this January. Critics often charge that Apollo was all about geopolitics and not about science. This is true on the merits, but it is also irrelevant. The inspiration summoned by Apollo was real, and the benefits to science and engineering are well documented in huge increases in graduate degrees and science careers. Still greater was the benefit to our common purpose.

Christa McAuliffe became a mother and a schoolteacher, and eventually an explorer and an inspiration to millions of children. I was one of them. Now I am part of a research team trying to slow climate change and deforestation, and my mom is still teaching.

Our hearts are in the stars.

> *"It may make sense to go to Venus before we ever send humans to Mars."*

Humans Should Begin Efforts to Colonize Venus

Evan Ackerman

Evan Ackerman is a writer for IEEE Spectrum. *In the following viewpoint, Ackerman contends that the atmosphere of Venus would provide ideal conditions for human colonization. This area is much like Earth's atmosphere, he writes, and could be traversed safely with large floating cities. Ackerman believes Venus should be explored in this way well before humans explore Mars for future habitation.*

As you read, consider the following questions:

1. What aspects of Venus's radiation and sun exposure does Ackerman say would benefit human colonization there?

2. How does Ackerman break down the length of time it would take for astronauts to travel to and study Venus?

3. What technologies does Ackerman's source say exploring Venus would help develop?

It has been accepted for decades that Mars is the next logical place for humans to explore. Mars certainly seems to offer the most Earth-like environment of any other place in the solar system, and it's closer to Earth than just about any place else, except Venus. But exploration of Venus has always been an enormous challenge: Venus's surface is hellish, with 92 atmospheres of pressure and temperatures of nearly 500°C.

The surface of Venus isn't going to work for humans, but what if we ignore the surface and stick to the clouds? Dale Arney and Chris Jones, from the Space Mission Analysis Branch of NASA's [National Aeronautics and Space Administration's] Systems Analysis and Concepts Directorate at Langley Research Center, in Virginia, have been exploring that idea. Perhaps humans could ride through the upper atmosphere of Venus in a solar-powered airship. Arney and Jones propose that it may make sense to go to Venus before we ever send humans to Mars.

To put NASA's High Altitude Venus Operational Concept (HAVOC) mission in context, it helps to start thinking about exploring the atmosphere of Venus instead of exploring the surface. "The vast majority of people, when they hear the idea of going to Venus and exploring, think of the surface, where it's hot enough to melt lead and the pressure is the same as if you were almost a mile underneath the ocean," Jones says. "I think that not many people have gone and looked at the relatively much more hospitable atmosphere and how you might tackle operating there for a while."

The Most Earth-like Environment

At 50 kilometers [km] above its surface, Venus offers one atmosphere of pressure and only slightly lower gravity than Earth. Mars, in comparison, has a "sea level" atmospheric pressure of less than a hundredth of Earth's, and gravity just over a third Earth normal. The temperature at 50 km on Venus is around 75°C, which is a mere 17 degrees hotter than the highest temperature recorded on Earth. It averages -63°C on Mars, and while neither extreme would be pleasant for an unprotected human, both are manageable.

What's more important, especially relative to Mars, is the amount of solar power available on Venus and the amount of protection that Venus has from radiation. The amount of radiation an astronaut would be exposed to in Venus's atmosphere would be "about the same as if you were in Canada," says Arney. On Mars, unshielded astronauts would be exposed to about 0.67 millisieverts [unit of measure for radiation absorption] per day, which is 40 times as much as on Earth, and they'd likely need to bury their habitats several meters beneath the surface to minimize exposure. As for solar power, proximity to the sun gets Venus 40 percent more than we get here on Earth, and 240 percent more than we'd see on Mars. Put all of these numbers together and as long as you don't worry about having something under your feet, Jones points out, the upper atmosphere of Venus is "probably the most Earth-like environment that's out there."

It's also important to note that Venus is often significantly closer to Earth than Mars is. Because of how the orbits of Venus and Earth align over time, a crewed mission to Venus would take a total of 440 days using existing or very near-term propulsion technology: 110 days out, a 30-day stay, and then 300 days back—with the option to abort and begin the trip back to Earth immediately after arrival. That sounds like a long time to spend in space, and it absolutely is. But getting to Mars and back using the same propulsive technology would involve more than 500 days in space at a minimum. A more realistic Mars mission would probably last anywhere from 650 to 900 days (or longer) due to the need to wait for a favorable orbital alignment for the return journey, which means that there's no option to abort the mission and come home earlier: If anything went wrong, astronauts would have to just wait around on Mars until their return window opened.

No Trivial Task

HAVOC comprises a series of missions that would begin by sending a robot into the atmosphere of Venus to check things out. That would be followed up by a crewed mission to Venus orbit with a stay of 30 days, and then a mission that includes a 30-day atmospheric stay. Later missions would have a crew of two spend a year in the atmosphere, and eventually there would be a permanent human presence there in a floating cloud city.

The defining feature of these missions is the vehicle that will be doing the atmospheric exploring: a helium-filled, solar-powered airship. The robotic version would be 31 meters long (about half the size of the Goodyear blimp), while the crewed version would be nearly 130 meters long, or twice the size of a Boeing 747. The top of the airship would be covered with more than 1,000 square meters of solar panels, with a gondola slung underneath for instruments and, in the crewed version, a small habitat and the ascent vehicle that the astronauts would use to return to Venus's orbit, and home.

Getting an airship to Venus is not a trivial task, and getting an airship to Venus with humans inside it is even more difficult. The crewed mission would involve a Venus orbit rendezvous, where the airship itself (folded up inside a spacecraft) would be sent to Venus ahead of time. Humans would follow in a transit vehicle (based on NASA's Deep Space Habitat), linking up with the airship in Venus orbit.

Since there's no surface to land on, the "landing" would be extreme, to say the least. "Traditionally, say if you're going to Mars, you talk about 'entry, descent, and landing,' or EDL," explains Arney. "Obviously, in our case, 'landing' would represent a significant failure of the mission, so instead we have 'entry, descent, and inflation,' or EDI." The airship would enter the Venusian atmosphere inside an aeroshell [a rigid outer shell that protects a spacecraft from heat, pressure, and debris] at 7,200 meters per second. Over the next seven minutes, the aeroshell would decelerate to 450 m/s [meters per second], and it would deploy a parachute to slow itself down further. At this point, things get crazy. The aeroshell would drop away, and the airship would begin to unfurl and inflate itself, while still dropping through the atmosphere at 100 m/s. As the airship got larger, its lift and drag would both increase to the point where the parachute became redundant. The parachute would be jettisoned, the airship would fully inflate, and (if everything had gone as it's supposed to), it would gently float to a stop at 50 km above Venus's surface.

Near the equator of Venus (where the atmosphere is most stable), winds move at about 100 meters per second, circling the planet in just 110 hours. Venus itself barely rotates, and one Venusian day takes longer than a Venusian year does. The slow day doesn't really matter, however, because for all practical purposes the 110-hour wind circumnavigation becomes the length of one day/night cycle. The winds also veer north, so to stay on course, the airship would push south during the day, when solar energy is plentiful, and drift north when it needs to conserve power at night.

Meanwhile, the humans would be busy doing science from inside a small (21-cubic-meter) habitat, based on NASA's existing Space Exploration Vehicle concept. There's not much reason to perform extravehicular activities, so that won't even be an option, potentially making things much simpler and safer (if a bit less exciting) than a trip to Mars.

The airship has a payload capacity of 70,000 kilograms [kg]. Of that, nearly 60,000 kg will be taken up by the ascent vehicle, a winged two-stage rocket slung below the airship. (If this looks familiar, it's because it's based on the much smaller Pegasus rocket, which is used to launch satellites into Earth orbit from beneath a carrier aircraft.) When it's time to head home, the astronauts would get into a tiny capsule on the front of the rocket, drop from the airship, and then blast back into orbit. There, they'll meet up with their transit vehicle and take it back to Earth orbit. The final stage is to rendezvous in Earth orbit with one final capsule (likely Orion), which the crew will use to make the return to Earth's surface.

The Future of HAVOC

The HAVOC team believes that its concept offers a realistic target for crewed exploration in the near future, pending moderate technological advancements and support from NASA. Little about HAVOC is dependent on technology that isn't near term. The primary restriction that a crewed version of HAVOC would face is that in its current incarnation it depends on the massive Block IIB configuration of the Space Launch System, which may not be ready to fly until the late 2020s. Several proof-of-concept studies have already been completed. These include testing Teflon coating that can protect solar cells (and other materials) from the droplets of concentrated sulfuric acid that are found throughout Venus's atmosphere and verifying that an airship with solar panels can be packed into an aeroshell and successfully inflated out of it, at least at 1/50 scale.

Many of the reasons that we'd want to go to Venus are identical to the reasons that we'd want to go to Mars, or anywhere else in the solar system, beginning with the desire to learn and explore. With the notable exception of the European Space Agency's Venus Express orbiter, the second planet from the sun has been largely ignored since the 1980s, despite its proximity and potential for scientific discovery. HAVOC, Jones says, "would be characterizing the environment not only for eventual human missions but also to understand the planet and how it's evolved and the runaway greenhouse effect and everything else that makes Venus so interesting." If the airships bring small robotic landers with them, HAVOC would complete many if not most of the science objectives that NASA's own Venus Exploration Analysis Group has been promoting for the past two decades.

"Venus has value as a destination in and of itself for exploration and colonization," says Jones. "But it's also complementary to current Mars plans.... There are things that you would need to do for a Mars mission, but we see a little easier path through Venus." For example, in order to get to Mars, or anywhere else outside of the Earth-moon system, we'll need experience with long-duration habitats, aerobraking and aerocapture, and carbon dioxide processing, among many other things. Arney continues: "If you did Venus first, you could get a leg up on advancing those technologies and those capabilities ahead of doing a human-scale Mars mission. It's a chance to do a practice run, if you will, of going to Mars."

It would take a substantial policy shift at NASA to put a crewed mission to Venus ahead of one to Mars, no matter how much sense it might make to take a serious look at HAVOC. But that in no way invalidates the overall concept for the mission, the importance of a crewed mission to Venus, or the vision of an eventual long-term human presence there in cities in the clouds. "If one does see humanity's future as expanding beyond just Earth, in all likelihood, Venus is probably no worse than the second planet you might go to behind Mars," says Arney. "Given that Venus's upper atmosphere is a fairly hospitable destination, we think it can play a role in humanity's future in space."

Periodical and Internet Sources Bibliography

The following articles have been selected to supplement the diverse views presented in this chapter.

Sarah Cruddas	"Mars One: 'We're All Going to Die, but It's Important What You Do Before You Die,'" CNN, February 18, 2015.
Bruce Dorminey	"Mars as a Hothouse for Offworld Human Culture," *Forbes*, March 30, 2015.
James Fallows	"The Coming Age of Space Colonization," *Atlantic*, March 20, 2013.
Matthew R. Francis	"What's Next for Space Exploration?," *Slate*, November 20, 2014.
Brian Fung	"The House Just Passed a Bill About Space Mining. The Future Is Here," *Washington Post*, May 22, 2015.
Jonathan Goff	"10 Reasons Why an Asteroid Redirect Mission Is Worth Doing," *SpaceNews*, February 16, 2015.
Richard Hollingham	"Five Steps to Colonising Mars," BBC, October 30, 2014.
K. Dean Larson	"Mining Asteroids and Exploiting the New Space Economy," *Wall Street Journal*, August 21, 2014.
Danielle N. Lee	"Colonize Mars? Not Until We Learn Some Lessons Here on Earth," Fusion, May 4, 2015.
Eric Mack	"Antares Explosion Won't Alter Long Road to Asteroid Mining," *Forbes*, October 29, 2014.
Jessica Orwig	"5 Undeniable Reasons Humans Need to Colonize Mars—Even Though It's Going to Cost Billions," Business Insider, April 21, 2015.

OPPOSING
VIEWPOINTS®
SERIES

CHAPTER 3

What Are the Politics of Space Exploration?

Chapter Preface

The United States' decision to retire its space shuttle program in 2011 generated enormous controversy among the American public. Some applauded the decision, as, in their eyes, it meant the federal government would stop funneling billions of dollars into the National Aeronautics and Space Administration (NASA), where the money disappeared into countless research projects that produced no tangible results. Others derided the move, claiming that by ending manned space missions, the United States would begin falling behind in the constant global push for technological advancement, allowing countries such as Russia and China to lead the world in space exploration.

Supporters of NASA's defunding countered by asserting what they claimed was a little-known fact about the early days of American spaceflight: that the Apollo program, which lasted from 1961 to 1975 and was responsible for landing the first humans on the moon in 1969, had been created only because of the geopolitical context of the Cold War that surrounded it. The Space Race was on between the United States and the Soviet Union, this faction argued, and it was this alone that had spurred such fantastic American space achievements in so short a time.

Within several years of the end of World War II in 1945, the Cold War began between the world's two superpowers, the United States and the Soviet Union. Not a war of actual combat, the Cold War was a period of dramatic tensions between the two nations to determine which form of government was superior: the free, capitalist democracy of the United States or the single-party Communist system of the Soviet Union. All aspects of the two societies were considered vital in this contest, from the governments themselves to their militaries and economies. Related to all of this was the development of technology, particularly for the exploration of space. Placing satellites, spacecraft, and humans in space was important to the two nations, not only for the glory of the achievements themselves but also to prove that each country was more militarily and economically robust than the other.

As fears of an American-Soviet nuclear war ran high in the late 1950s, the Soviet Union made its first leap forward in the Space Race in 1957 by using an intercontinental ballistic missile to launch Sputnik, the first man-made satellite ever to be placed in Earth's orbit. The launch greatly disturbed the American public, for it meant the Soviet Union was now capable of firing nuclear missiles at the United States from outer space. In response, the United States launched Explorer I, its own first satellite, in 1958. That year, to galvanize further such accomplishments, President Dwight Eisenhower created NASA.

In April 1961, the Soviet Union again pulled ahead of the United States by launching a spacecraft carrying Soviet astronaut, or cosmonaut, Yuri Gagarin into space, making him the first human ever to leave Earth's atmosphere. American astronaut Alan Shepard became a close second when *Freedom 7* was launched a month later. In 1961 President John F. Kennedy created the Apollo program to accomplish what was considered an even greater space feat than anything that had yet occurred: putting humans on the moon. At the end of the decade, after much research and development resulting from a federal budget increase of five hundred percent, NASA's 1969 Apollo 11 mission landed astronauts Neil Armstrong and Edwin "Buzz" Aldrin Jr. on the moon, allowing them to become the first humans ever to walk on the moon. The American moon landing was considered a great Space Race victory over the Soviet Union, which never successfully placed humans on the moon before its dissolution in 1991.

The following chapter presents viewpoints exploring the politics of contemporary space exploration. Topics discussed include the future of the private space industry, the question of manned American spaceflight, and China's potential threats to the United States from outer space.

> "Only the private sector has people will-
> ing to take losses for years, and often
> be ruined, for the chance to succeed be-
> yond imagination."

Private Industry Is the Future of Space Exploration

Andrew L. Peek

Andrew L. Peek is a doctoral candidate at Johns Hopkins University's Paul H. Nitze School of Advanced International Studies. In the following viewpoint, Peek argues that the private space industry will lead humanity's advancement into new reaches of space exploration. The National Aeronautics and Space Administration (NASA) is nearly obsolete, he claims, while corporations such as SpaceX plan on putting people on Mars. To Peek, this clearly exemplifies that individuals should look to private industry for developments in space travel.

As you read, consider the following questions:

1. Peeks say the new space race should be about what?

Andrew L. Peek, "The New Space Race, and Why Nothing Else Matters," Thefiscal times.com, July 11, 2014. © 2014 Fiscal Times. This column first appears on July 11, 2014, in *The Fiscal Times*, which owns the copyright. Reproduced by permission.

2. What incentive does Peek suggest for convincing corporations to invest in space development?

3. Under what three conditions does Peek suggest the United States defend the interests of space entrepreneurs?

Forty-five years ago this July 20th [2014], Neil Armstrong and Buzz Aldrin became the first human beings to set foot on the moon. Their mission represented an emphatic American victory in the first Space Race, which began in earnest in 1957 when the Soviet Union launched a notably unattractive satellite, Sputnik, into orbit.

Since then, however, America's national space program has essentially foundered. It improved space travel by building and then scrapping the space shuttle, without ever accomplishing—or attempting—a mission as bold or impactful as the one in 1969. It's time for a new one. To win the next space race, the U.S. should announce its support for private property rights in space, and NASA [National Aeronautics and Space Administration] should take a back seat.

To be fair, NASA's not really at fault here: Its business model is just wrong. In the national consciousness, NASA seems like a luxury, in the same low-priority bucket as the F-22A fighter and development aid for Bosnia. And unlike those other items, it's not really clear what the last thirty years of NASA funding has given us. As America's government-run space monopoly, NASA is a money hole, no more viable over the long run than is Amtrak.

That's a shame, because we're not far off from the next major iteration of space exploration. Tesla Motors and SpaceX CEO [chief executive officer] Elon Musk believes that humans could be travelling to Mars within 10–12 years. And former NASA official and Stanford [University] astronautics professor

G. Scott Hubbard sees private space exploration for tourism, residency, or resource extraction as goals for the next iteration of space travel.

That's the new space race: not tourism, not residency *per se*, but resource extraction.

According to some estimates, a single half-kilometer asteroid could contain over $20 trillion worth of metals and other resources.

The first nation that can import and tax the raw materials of bodies in our solar system would experience an economic boom unparalleled in generations, if ever.

In addition, the military-technological spillover advantages from a vastly expanded space industry might never be surpassed. Since space is infinite, there's no limit to how far the mining sector can expand—the bounds of the solar system in the short term, but in the longer term, who knows? It would be a period of international growth and change unseen since the Age of Discovery, when Spain and Portugal broke out of the European system and became superpowers almost overnight. And, like the 1400s, the first country up there will win.

The Space Future

But only private industry will risk it. Only the private sector has people willing to take losses for years, and often be ruined, for the chance to succeed beyond imagination.

The [Barack] Obama administration's 2010 space strategy, which encouraged commercial firms to develop the capability to fly U.S. astronauts into space, did recognize that private industry will be the driver of space exploration. The problem, however, is that human launch capability is not that intrinsically valuable a service.

True, we need it to put astronauts into the International Space Station, where they produce marginally valuable scientific research and watch the World Cup. But that still falls into the "expensive curiosity" label that killed the space shuttle.

Google Takes on Space

Google Inc. is close to investing roughly $1 billion in Space Exploration Technologies Corporation [SpaceX] to support its nascent efforts to deliver Internet access via satellites, according to a person familiar with the matter.

The investment would value SpaceX, backed by Tesla Motors Inc. chief executive Elon Musk, at more than $10 billion, according to this person. It isn't clear what exact stake Google could end up with in the fast-growing space company.

If Google completes the deal, it would be the Internet company's latest effort to use futuristic technology to spread Internet access to remote regions of the world, alongside high-altitude balloons and solar-powered drones. By extending Web access, Google increases the number of people who can use its services. . . .

SpaceX builds and launches rockets and spacecraft. Mr. Musk last week described a general concept for SpaceX to launch hundreds of satellites into relatively low orbit to deliver Internet access across the globe. Mr. Musk told *BusinessWeek* the project could cost $10 billion to build and take at least five years, but gave no details about funding or manufacturing plans.

For several months Mr. Musk has been mulling ways to expand SpaceX's rocket-and-spacecraft manufacturing operations to designing and building satellites, according to aerospace-industry officials who have talked with him. Though short on specifics, his latest comments were the clearest sign yet of a long-term commitment to such expansion plans.

Rolfe Winkler, Evelyn Rusli, and Andy Pasztor,
"Google Nears $1 Billion Investment in SpaceX,"
Wall Street Journal, *January 19, 2015.*

Even a human visit to Mars or a permanent human presence on the moon would not be much more than a milestone for the human race, which—though laudable—is not the most alluring incentive for government or private cash.

But what if space exploration companies could be offered property rights for the resources they extract as well? Private property rights are a mainstay of economic development theory. This would in one stroke encourage far-seeing corporations to invest in space development projects that are virtually guaranteed to have a long-term (indeed, almost infinite) reward.

One that's already in the market is Planetary Resources, a new asteroid-mining company supported in part by Google's CEOs Larry Page and Eric Schmidt. Given the right policy support, others would be quick to join it. Then it's California in 1849, and the gold rush is on.

America's Place

The U.S. should thus make an explicit promise to space entrepreneurs: If they pay U.S. taxes, follow to-be-created U.S. environmental regulations, and share their technology with the government, the government will defend their claim diplomatically and legally. NASA in this model would play the role of a regulator and information repository, and possibly an R&D [research and development] lab for U.S. companies.

They'd need it, because other countries would be upset. Operating in the quirky netherworld of never-put-to-the-test space law, the U.S. would be essentially creating customary law on the fly. To smooth the transition, it could also offer a diplomatic incentive: that it would defend the claims of foreign companies whose countries recognize U.S. claims.

That would be a powerful inducement to cooperate in the new space race. Most likely, after initial responses ranging from ridicule to Brazil-level meltdown, the most developed U.S. allies like Japan, Germany, and the Anglosphere [English-speaking nations with a similar cultural heritage] would follow suit, either alone or in alliances with companies from the developing world.

Because, if it works, everything else looks like pawn-grabbing. The frontiers of Ukraine, China's claim to Pacific atolls, even the vast caldron of inchoate sectarian rage in the Middle East: strategically, all would have less of a long-term impact than the economic and technological benefits of space mining. The first countries to do it successfully will be the superpowers of the space age—and the last may disappear.

And if it goes nowhere, then so what? The U.S. has lost nothing except some diplomatic angst.

There's always more where that came from.

"[Neil] Armstrong feared becoming reliant on other nations for spaceflight and that private companies would take too long to develop new space-worthy vehicles."

Privatized Space Exploration Has Disadvantages and Benefits

Agence France-Presse

Agence France-Presse is an international news agency based in Paris. In the following viewpoint, the author writes that famed American astronaut Neil Armstrong greatly doubted the abilities of private space companies to compete with government space programs. The agency reports that in 2010 Armstrong criticized the Barack Obama administration's cost-cutting plans to end the US space shuttle program, a move that took Americans out of space. Armstrong believed that private industry was too slow at developing new technologies, and he aligned instead with the National Aeronautics and Space Administration (NASA), which defended its space exploration missions.

As you read, consider the following questions:

1. What factors does the author's source say brought about the rise of the Apollo space program?

2. How much of the federal budget did NASA receive at the time of the moon landing, according to the author?

3. According to the viewpoint, what two factors will allow for greater human achievements in space?

More than 40 years after Neil Armstrong landed on the moon, humans continue to push the frontiers of space exploration but missions are being tempered by costs, a trend that concerned the astronaut.

The blank check from government that financed adventures in the Cold War [nonviolent post–World War II conflict between the United States and the Soviet Union] era is no longer available, with today's missions depending more on the private sector and international cooperation—often because of budget considerations.

Armstrong, who died Saturday [August 25, 2012], criticized President Barack Obama in 2010 for cost-cutting plans that, in part, retired the US space shuttles—effectively ending the American role in sending humans out of Earth's orbit.

Space Exploration Evolution

Now, US astronauts—whose predecessors worked feverishly to beat Russia's efforts to the moon—ride as passengers on Russian spacecraft, and hopes for NASA's [National Aeronautics and Space Administration's] own future manned flights to the International Space Station are pinned on private companies, which are trying to build cheaper shuttle alternatives.

Armstrong feared becoming reliant on other nations for spaceflight and that private companies would take too long to develop new space-worthy vehicles.

"I support the encouragement of the newcomers toward their goal of lower cost access to space," Armstrong said. "But having cut my teeth in rockets more than 50 years ago, I am not confident."

US analysts, however, say the country's space program had no choice but to change, given new global realities.

"The world evolves, humanity evolves, our capabilities evolve. And the future of space exploration, therefore, must also evolve," said Jeff Foust, an aerospace consultant and the editor of TheSpaceReview.com.

For one thing, flights into low Earth orbit are now routine, and privatizing them allows the space agency to focus its efforts on more cutting-edge missions, according to Foust.

But there are no footsteps on Mars, and many other hopes that were dreamed of when Armstrong and Apollo 11 crewmate Buzz Aldrin helped mankind make its "giant leap" in 1969 are still unrealized.

Foust said the succeed-at-any-cost mentality that drove the Apollo program to get the first person on the moon cannot be replicated.

That program "was the result of the particular geopolitical factors, that Cold War atmosphere," Foust explained.

"We need to find different approaches that can be sustained, probably at lower funding levels than we had under Apollo, but over longer periods of time," he added.

Cuts and Consequences

Roger Launius, senior curator and historian at the Smithsonian National Air and Space Museum, noted that Obama's cuts at NASA follow two decades of financial slashing since the Cold War ended.

At the height of the moon-landing effort, NASA was allocated fully five percent of the federal budget, Launius told AFP [Agence France-Presse].

For much of the 1970s and 1980s, NASA's share stayed steady at one percent, he explained, but "today it's less than one half of one percent of the federal budget."

Still Launius insisted the US space program continues to make important gains—not least of which was landing the Curiosity rover on Mars last month [August 2012].

Over the next decade, Launius said, "we're going to send robots literally all over the solar system. We're doing that now. And we're going to learn more about the cosmos. We're also sending robots and satellites into space to monitor Earth to understand what's happening here.

"That's not personal jet packs. And it's not colonies on the moon. It's not *The Jetsons*," he joked, referring to a once popular cartoon about a space-age family. "But it is very real and very important."

These missions, however, have often failed to stoke the public's imagination the way Apollo's astronauts once did.

One consequence is a ricochet effect on NASA's ability to do the bigger more ambitious projects that do inspire people, said Keith Cowing, a former NASA employee and editor at NASAWatch.com, an unaffiliated website following the agency's activities.

"NASA needs to be able to tell its story far better than it does. If people truly understood what space exploration is about, and the promise that it offers, they'd be clamoring to triple NASA's budget," he said.

Barring that, Foust said international cooperation and private sector gains will allow greater achievements all around.

"International partnerships"—like the ones behind the International Space Station—"give us the tool to do things that would be more difficult or impossible for individual nations to do," he said.

Such a model will likely form the basis of future human space exploration, "particularly the really big and expensive missions like sending people to Mars."

> "It is long past time that NASA has the budget needed to reinstate the space exploration program."

The United States Should Reignite the Space Race

Erin Wallace

Erin Wallace is a writer for the Daily Toreador, *the student newspaper of Texas Tech University. In the following viewpoint, Wallace argues that the United States should reinvigorate the National Aeronautics and Space Administration (NASA) so Americans can create a lasting legacy of space exploration. To do this, the government must vote to increase NASA funding, she writes, as only this will generate a respectable image of American science and engineering.*

As you read, consider the following questions:

1. What three reasons does the Smithsonian National Air and Space Museum give for the United States going to space again?

2. How much does Wallace say NASA should receive annually from the federal budget?

3. How does Wallace's source suggest Americans become involved in convincing the government to provide more support to NASA?

The recent success of the movie *Interstellar* [in 2014] has reignited a passion for space exploration in people around the world. The film, starring Academy Award winners Matthew McConaughey and Anne Hathaway, raked in $132 million worldwide in its opening weekend. The movie even sparked interest from world-renowned cosmologist Neil deGrasse Tyson.

People around the world have always admired space exploration, but Americans especially have taken an interest in it. Who hasn't been inspired by Neil Armstrong walking across the moon and saying, "One small step for man, one giant leap for mankind?"

Space exploration in the United States, according to Space .com, ended in 2011 after the space shuttle *Endeavour* returned back to Earth. This was a travesty to the scientific community, but even more so, a major blow to the American public. Since space exploration began, astronauts have been considered the bravest and the noblest Americans. In losing out on space exploration, astronauts could no longer explore space in the same way and try to understand why we exist and what/who else is out there.

According to an article by the *Huffington Post*, "The nation that put humans on the moon and inspired generations of excellence in science, technology, engineering and math is now paying Russia to transport Americans to and from the International Space Station. And we wonder why U.S. students are falling behind in science, technology, engineering, and math. With a lack of clear objectives widely supported by the public, the government, and industry, has the United States human

Space Exploration and American Competitiveness

The Soviet Union took the world by surprise in October 1957 with the launch of Sputnik, the first artificial satellite. In a matter of months, President Dwight D. Eisenhower and Congress initiated measures to build U.S. scientific and engineering prowess, including the creation of NASA, a civilian space exploration agency. . . .

After six successful lunar missions, NASA's manned program pulled back to Earth, while robotic missions such as Voyager and Viking continued to explore the solar system. NASA focused on sending astronauts into low Earth orbit (LEO) with the 1973 launch of Skylab, the first U.S. space station, and the space shuttle. The space shuttle served NASA for thirty years (1981–2011) and helped build the International Space Station (ISS), an orbiting laboratory that has been continuously occupied by humans since 2000. . . .

Space exploration is expensive, but it is a relatively minor line item in the U.S. budget. NASA's spending peaked at almost 4.5 percent of the federal budget in fiscal year (FY) 1966, declined to 1 percent by 1975, and has gradually fallen to about half a percent in recent years. . . .

The [Barack] Obama administration's FY 2015 budget proposal for NASA is $17.5 billion, just below the $17.7 billion appropriated for FY 2014. Major expenditures include science missions ($5 billion), space operations such as the ISS ($3.9 billion), and new commercial and public exploration development ($4 billion).

Steven J. Markovich,
"Space Exploration and U.S. Competitiveness,"
Council on Foreign Relations, December 5, 2014.

spaceflight program, once the symbol of excellence and inno-vation throughout the world, been relegated to history books?"

Innovation and Chances

It is long past time that NASA [National Aeronautics and Space Administration] has the budget needed to reinstate the space exploration program.

According to the Smithsonian [National] Air and Space Museum website, we go to space "for purposes of scientific discovery, economic benefit and national security." We are also a society that values innovation and taking chances to achieve.

The [National] Air and Space Museum website cites three reasons we need to go to space: to be the best, to satisfy curi-osity and to leave a legacy behind. "Most of us want to be, both as individuals and as societies, the first or the best in some activity. We want to stand out. This behavior is rooted in our genes. We are today the descendants of people who survived by outperforming others," according to the website.

The most significant of the three reasons is about our de-sire to leave a legacy behind. Do we want to be known as the generation that stopped American space exploration? We are, as of now, the generation of people that ended decades of in-novation and education about the universe and our place in it. We cannot leave this behind for our children or grandchil-dren.

According to the [National] Air and Space Museum web-site, "We want to leave something behind to show the next generation, or the generations after that, what we did with our time here."

The need to fund space exploration again, of course, comes with a very high price tag. NASA, according to Save Our Sci-ence, needs to receive $1.5 billion per budgetary year. "Right now the White House proposes far less than that ($1.28

billion)," for the budget of 2015. To keep this money in context, $1.5 billion is "less overall than what Americans spent on dog toys in 2012."

An organization called Penny4NASA spreads awareness of the budget crisis NASA is facing. "NASA's current budget, at 0.5 percent of the total U.S. budget, does not reflect the hugely important economic, technological and inspirational resource that this agency has been in its 50+ year history. This is the people saying that as a society, we want our tax dollars to reflect the importance of scientific exploration, research and education; and 0.5 percent doesn't cut it. The NASA budget must be increased to at least 1 percent of the U.S. federal budget," according to Penny4NASA's website.

This organization is urging Americans to get involved and start to fight for NASA. According to the website, . . . ways citizens can help are "a high number of supporters which can be contacted quickly to act as one voice at the same time; a public presence that consistently reminds the administration and Congress that we want our society to support NASA funding at a higher level, concurrent with the agency's economical, technological and inspirational excellence; and perhaps most importantly, by consistently and in large numbers, contacting members of Congress to tell them what we want and why we want it."

It is long past time the U.S. reinstates its space exploration program. Space travel is the epitome of scientific exploration and the necessity of curiosity. We can all get involved in spreading the word about raising the budget to fund NASA. The U.S. was built on the idea of leaving behind a legacy—we need space exploration and we need NASA at its full capacity.

"Entrepreneurs are far more likely to find inspiration down in the depths of the ocean than up in the heavens."

The United States Should Invest in Oceans Before Space

Michael Conathan

Michael Conathan is director of ocean policy at the Center for American Progress. In the following viewpoint, Conathan argues that exploration of the world's oceans deserves more attention and funding than space exploration. The oceans still contain much to discover and learn from, he believes, estimating that scientists still have not discovered more than 90 percent of the species that inhabit Earth's oceans. Conathan contends that while space exploration is exciting and supported in popular culture and by an exorbitant amount of government funding, it offers humans few tangible benefits.

As you read, consider the following questions:

1. What percentage of the world's oceans does Conathan claim humans have seen?

2. What important benefits does Conathan say the ocean provides to humans?

3. What does Conathan suggest the United States do to claim the opportunity to lead the world in ocean exploration?

Star Trek would have us believe that space is the final frontier, but with apologies to the armies of Trekkies, their oracle might be a tad off base. Though we know little about outer space, we still have plenty of frontiers to explore here on our home planet. And they're losing the race of discovery.

Hollywood giant James Cameron, director of megablockbusters such as *Titanic* and *Avatar*, brought this message to Capitol Hill last week [in June 2013], along with the single-seat submersible that he used to become the third human to journey to the deepest point of the world's oceans—the Marianas Trench. By contrast, more than 500 people have journeyed into space—including Sen. Bill Nelson (D-FL), who sits on the committee before which Cameron testified—and 12 people have actually set foot on the surface of the moon.

All it takes is a quick comparison of the budgets for NASA [National Aeronautics and Space Administration] and the National Oceanic and Atmospheric Administration, or NOAA, to understand why space exploration is outpacing its ocean counterpart by such a wide margin.

Incongruous Access

In fiscal year 2013, NASA's annual exploration budget was roughly $3.8 billion. That same year, total funding for everything NOAA does—fishery management, weather and climate forecasting, ocean research and management, among many other programs—was about $5 billion, and NOAA's Office of Exploration and Research received just $23.7 million. Something is wrong with this picture.

Space travel is certainly expensive. But as Cameron proved with his dive that cost approximately $8 million, deep-sea exploration is pricey as well. And that's not the only similarity between space and ocean travel: Both are dark, cold, and completely inhospitable to human life.

Yet space travel excites Americans' imaginations in a way ocean exploration never has. To put this in terms Cameron may be familiar with, just think of how stories are told on screens both big and small: Space dominates, with *Star Trek*, *Star Wars*, *Battlestar Galactica*, *Buck Rogers in the 25th Century*, and *2001: A Space Odyssey*. Then there are B-movies such as *Plan 9 from Outer Space* and everything ever mocked on *Mystery Science Theater 3000*. There are even parodies: *Spaceballs*, *Galaxy Quest*, and *Mars Attacks!* And let's not forget Cameron's own contributions: *Aliens* and *Avatar*.

When it comes to the ocean, we have *20,000 Leagues Under the Sea*, *SpongeBob SquarePants*, and Cameron's somewhat lesser-known film *The Abyss*. And that's about it.

This imbalance in pop culture is illustrative of what plays out in real life. We rejoiced along with the NASA mission-control room when the Mars rover landed on the red planet late last year. One particularly exuberant scientist, known as "Mohawk Guy" for his audacious hairdo, became a minor celebrity and even fielded his share of spontaneous marriage proposals. But when Cameron bottomed out in the Challenger Deep more than 36,000 feet below the surface of the sea, it was met with resounding indifference from all but the dorkiest of ocean nerds such as myself.

Part of this incongruity comes from access. No matter where we live, we can go outside on a clear night, look up into the sky, and wonder about what's out there. We're presented with a spectacular vista of stars, planets, meteorites, and even the occasional comet or aurora. We have all been wishing on stars since we were children. Only the lucky few can gaze out at the ocean from their doorstep, and even those who do cannot see all that lies beneath the waves.

As a result, the facts about ocean exploration are pretty bleak. Humans have laid eyes on less than 5 percent of the ocean, and we have better maps of the surface of Mars than we do of America's exclusive economic zone—the undersea territory reaching out 200 miles from our shores.

Prioritizing Dollars

Sure, space is sexy. But the oceans are, too. To those intrigued by the quest for alien life, consider this: Scientists estimate that we still have not discovered 91 percent of the species that live in our oceans. And some of them look pretty outlandish. Go ahead and Google the deep-sea hatchetfish, frilled shark, or *Bathynomus giganteus*.

In a time of shrinking budgets and increased scrutiny on the return for our investments, we should be taking a long, hard look at how we are prioritizing our exploration dollars. If the goal of government spending is to spur growth in the private sector, entrepreneurs are far more likely to find inspiration down in the depths of the ocean than up in the heavens. The ocean already provides us with about half the oxygen we breathe, our single largest source of protein, a wealth of mineral resources, key ingredients for pharmaceuticals, and marine biotechnology.

Of course space exploration does have benefits beyond the "cool factor" of putting people on the moon and astronaut-bards playing David Bowie covers in space. Inventions created to facilitate space travel have become ubiquitous in our lives— cell phone cameras, scratch-resistant lenses, and water filtration systems, just to name a few—and research conducted in outer space has led to breakthroughs here on Earth in the technological and medical fields. Yet despite far-fetched plans

Earth's Oceans

Earth is the only known planet or moon to have large bodies of liquid water on its surface. Our planet lies in the "Goldilocks" zone—not too hot, not too cold and with enough atmospheric pressure to prevent liquid surface water from evaporating into space. . . .

Our oceans teem with life ranging from the blue whale—the biggest animal on Earth—to tiny microbes.

But nobody knows exactly how many different species live in this environment. There is no data for around 20 per cent of the ocean's volume.

The Census of Marine Life, a 10-year international project to identify life in our oceans, found nearly 250,000 species. But scientists believe at least a million species of marine life could be out there, and that's not counting the tens or even hundreds of millions of kinds of microbes that make up the majority of marine life.

What we do know is that ocean life survives in the most extreme environments. Scientists have found life that can survive in temperatures that melt lead, where seawater freezes into ice, or [where] there's no light or oxygen.

In fact, the dark ocean zone between 1000 and 5000 metres known as the abyssal zone has a far greater range of marine life than we once thought.

The deep waters around Australia's Great Barrier Reef are home to a stunning array of life such as the deep-sea jellyfish Atolla, which was discovered by Australian scientists in 2006.

"10 Facts About Our Amazing Oceans,"
ABC Science, June 4, 2014.

to mine asteroids for rare metals, the only tangible goods brought back from space to date remain a few piles of moon rocks.

The deep seabed is a much more likely source of so-called rare earth metals than distant asteroids. Earlier this year, the United Nations [U.N.] published its first plan for management of mineral resources beneath the high seas that are outside the jurisdiction of any individual country. The United States has not been able to participate in negotiations around this policy because we are not among the 185 nations that have ratified the U.N. Convention on the Law of the Sea, which governs such activity.

With or without the United States on board, the potential for economic development in the most remote places on the planet is vast and about to leap to the next level. Earlier this year, Japan announced that it has discovered a massive supply of rare earth both within its exclusive economic zone and in international waters. This follows reports in 2011 that China sent at least one exploratory mission to the seabed beneath international waters in the Pacific Ocean. There is a real opportunity for our nation to lead in this area, but we must invest and join the rest of the world in creating the governance structure for these activities.

Toward the end of last week's hearing, Sen. Mark Begich (D-AK), who chairs the Subcommittee on Oceans, Atmosphere, Fisheries, and Coast Guard, hypothetically asked where we would be today if we had spent half as much money exploring the oceans as we have spent exploring space. Given the current financial climate in Congress, we won't find the answer to his question on Capitol Hill.

But there may be another way.

Cameron is currently in preproduction on the second and third *Avatar* films. He says the former will be set on an ocean planet. No one except he and his fellow producers at 20th Century Fox really knows how much the first installment of the movie series cost, but estimates peg it at approximately $250 million—or 10 times the total funding for NOAA's Ocean Exploration program. Since the original *Avatar* grossed more than $2 billion at the box office worldwide, if NASA isn't willing to hand over a bit of its riches to help their oceanic co-explorers, maybe Cameron and his studio partners can chip a percent or two off the gross from *Avatar 2* to help fill the gap.

Come to think of it, if the key to exploring the oceans hinges either on Hollywood giving up profits or Congress increasing spending, maybe we are more likely to mine asteroids after all.

"*Anti-satellite missiles are one of the most serious threats to space assets.*"

China's Space Program Threatens the United States

Yasmin Tadjdeh

Yasmin Tadjdeh is a writer for National Defense *magazine. In the following viewpoint, Tadjdeh argues that continued Chinese technological development could one day pose a military threat to American satellites in space. She claims that this was demonstrated in China's 2007 destruction of one of its own orbiting weather satellites. The US military will need to take precautions to ensure space warfare with China does not occur, Tadjdeh concludes.*

As you read, consider the following questions:

1. According to Tadjdeh, what orbital tracking system did the US Air Force contract Lockheed Martin to create?

2. What distance above Earth qualifies as low Earth orbit, according to the viewpoint?

3. According to Tadjdeh, the twenty-three thousand Earth-orbiting objects that the military tracks in space break down into what categories?

Last year [2013], China launched a mysterious missile from its southwest region. While Chinese news sources said it was a scientific experiment, there is widespread speculation that the payload was a more advanced anti-satellite test.

Satellites are vulnerable to an array of weapons and disruptive technologies like anti-satellite missiles and sophisticated cyber attacks that can have potentially devastating results from degrading capabilities to complete annihilation, experts said.

There is strong evidence that the anti-satellite weapon China tested in May 2013 went higher than low Earth orbit, said Charles Miller, president of NextGen Space LLC, a space and public policy consulting group. If China continues to make strides and develops weapons that reach farther, it could one day threaten key satellites in geosynchronous orbit.

Military Utility

The damage caused by an anti-satellite missile is twofold: Not only does it destroy its target, but it also causes a massive ripple effect with debris from the collision striking other satellites. China's 2007 test created a large debris field, which could damage other spacecraft, said Gen. William Shelton, commander of Air Force Space Command.

The Air Force in June took new steps to better track and observe man-made debris in space. The service awarded Lockheed Martin a $915 million contract to develop the Space Fence, which has been in the works for years and is now entering final system development with the delivery of increment 1 and an operations center. The system will track objects in low Earth orbit and some in higher orbits. The Air Force plans to have the system operational by 2019, and the contract leaves open the possibility for a second radar site.

In February, Director of National Intelligence James R. Clapper said potential adversaries are hard at work developing weapons that could degrade or destroy some of the United States' key satellites that provide essential communication to the military, the government and U.S. citizens.

"Threats to U.S. space services will increase during 2014 and beyond, as potential adversaries pursue disruptive and destructive counter-space capabilities," Clapper told the Senate Armed Services Committee [SASC]. "Chinese and Russian military leaders understand the unique information advantages afforded by space systems and are developing capabilities to disrupt the United States' use of space in a conflict."

In the months since his testimony, top U.S. military officials and policy analysts have echoed the same concern. As U.S. dependence on satellites grows, so does the vulnerability of its space assets.

Satellites beam essential information down to Earth. From mapping services to phone calls to Internet access, both the military and civilian world rely on timely and secure connections. The armed services use GPS [global positioning system] satellites to guide unmanned aerial vehicles, missiles and other weapons. Reconnaissance satellites track enemy movements.

The military utility of satellite technology cannot be understated, said Shelton. Capabilities provided by satellites help the military conduct humanitarian, disaster relief and combat operations, he said.

"In space, our sustained mission success integrating these [satellite] capabilities into our military operations has encouraged potential adversaries to further develop counter-space technologies and attempt to exploit our systems and information. Therefore, I believe we are at a strategic crossroad in space," Shelton said before the SASC in March.

"We are so dependent on space these days. We plug into it like a utility. It is always there. Nobody worries about it," Shelton said. "You do not even know sometimes that you are touching space. So [to lose our space capabilities] it would be almost a reversion back to . . . industrial-based warfare."

Bill Ostrove, a space systems analyst at Forecast International, a Newtown, Connecticut–based marketing and consulting firm, agreed that the military stands to lose much in the event of an attack on satellite systems.

"If satellites are knocked out, even temporarily, it could have serious consequences on the military's ability to operate effectively," Ostrove said.

Anti-satellite missiles are one of the most serious threats to space assets, he said.

"There are a few different ways that a satellite could be disabled that the United States is afraid of. The most obvious way is to launch a missile into space that targets a satellite," Ostrove said. "The United States has a legitimate fear of anti-satellite weapons."

A Dangerous Precedent

In 2007, China successfully launched an anti-satellite missile into low Earth orbit and destroyed one of its aging weather satellites.

The test is concerning because it means China could potentially target a U.S. satellite in low Earth orbit. The U.S. military is monitoring China's development of the weapons, Shelton said.

"We are concerned about low Earth orbit because we saw the 2007 Chinese ASAT [anti-satellite weapons] test, which was a success," Shelton said. "We are concerned about work that we have seen since then that includes all the way up to geosynchronous orbit. Some of our most precious assets fly in geosynchronous orbit."

Low Earth orbit is defined as 160 to 2,000 kilometers above Earth's surface. Most spacecraft fly in it, as does the International Space Station. Satellites in geosynchronous orbit fly about 36,000 kilometers above Earth's equator.

China's Space Program

China by virtue of the ambition of its space program stands out.

Already, it has managed to land a rover on the moon and to return an unmanned spacecraft from orbiting the moon as part of its preparation for an eventual manned landing. It also aims to have a manned space station operational by 2020.

China is a relatively new actor among the traditional space powers, the Soviet Union and the United States. The quest to conquer space was driven from the middle of the 20th century by the rivalry between them. National pride was inextricably linked to the early achievements of getting a man into space and landing on the moon. . . .

China has already achieved rapid success and has more long-term plans for deeper venturing into space including to Mars.

Louis Brennan,
"New World Order in Space—Why China Stands Out,"
CNN, May 29, 2015.

As for the 2013 test, it was likely disguised as a research experiment, Miller said, citing a study by the Secure World Foundation, a Broomfield, Colorado–based private foundation that works to keep space sustainable. The rocket reached more than 10,000 kilometers in altitude and then released a canister of barium powder, the report found.

The test is alarming because satellites in geosynchronous orbit are vulnerable, Miller said in May during a panel discussion on space threats at the American Security Project, a Washington, D.C.–based think tank.

"Most of the United States' assets in space for national security are in geosynchronous orbit. They are completely fragile," Miller said.

The advanced extremely high-frequency system, which provides the U.S. and allied militaries with secure communications, is one example of a key satellite that flies in the orbit and could one day be targeted by adversaries.

Xinhua, China's state-run news service, said the May 2013 rocket was launched from the Xichang Satellite Launch Center in southwest China and meant to "investigate energetic particles and magnetic fields in the ionized stratum and near-Earth space."

A U.S.-China Economic and Security Review Commission paper, titled "China Missile Launch May Have Tested Part of a New Anti-Satellite Capability," said if the launch was indeed an anti-satellite test and not a research experiment, it would show that China is not being transparent about its space objectives. It may also signal that China is attempting to develop weapons that could destroy crucial U.S. satellites, it said.

"Such a test would signal China's intent to develop an ASAT capability to target satellites in an altitude range that includes U.S. GPS and many U.S. military and intelligence satellites," the report said. "In a conflict, this could allow China to threaten the U.S. military's ability to detect foreign missiles and provide secure communications, navigation and precision missile guidance."

China's 2007 test created 3,000 new pieces of debris, according to the National Security Space Strategy of 2011, the Defense Department's most recent guidance on space issues. Another 1,500 pieces of debris were created when a Russian and U.S. satellite collided in 2009.

The military tracks about 23,000 objects in orbit, Shelton said. About 1,000 of them are active payloads, and the rest include defunct satellites, pieces of debris and other items, he said.

Military sensors generally can track objects that are larger than 10 centimeters across, Shelton said. However, there could be 500,000 man-made objects in orbit that are smaller than that and can cause significant damage to satellites, he said.

The military is also working to ensure that adversaries do not attack satellites through cyber intrusions, Shelton said.

"We are going system by system looking at our cyber vulnerabilities, and we have a large information assurance program that gets into those vulnerabilities and patches them and tries to prevent access," he said. "In many cases, these are closed systems. That does not mean there are not vulnerabilities, but they are . . . not accessible through the Internet. So it would take insider—special access—those kinds of things to get to these closed networks."

Some countries, such as China, are also developing technologies that use lasers to "dazzle" a satellite, said Micah Walter-Range, director of research and analysis at the Space Foundation, a Colorado Springs–based advocacy group. By shining lasers at the craft, adversaries overload the satellite's sensors and can temporarily blind or permanently damage it, he said.

Mitigating Attacks and Vulnerabilities

While a degradation of the capabilities provided by the nation's space assets would hurt the military, it would also be detrimental for the general public, said Mariel Borowitz, an assistant professor at the Sam Nunn School of International Affairs at the Georgia Institute of Technology, who studies space issues. Television, Internet access, radio and telephone service could go dark, she said.

"The threat to satellite technology is serious. The United States has more satellites than any other country in the world, and satellite technologies are critical to both our economic system and our military," Borowitz said.

Economically, the country relies on GPS for logistical, agricultural and safety applications. Boaters and pilots also rely heavily on weather satellites, Borowitz said.

The U.S. government is looking at numerous ways to prevent and mitigate attacks or vulnerabilities.

Disaggregation, which takes one large satellite and splits it into smaller spacecraft, is one way to protect satellite capabilities, Shelton said. If an enemy attacks the system and takes out a few satellites, there will still be some functionality left, he said.

"By separating payloads on different satellites we will complicate a potential adversary's targeting calculus, decrease size and system complexity and enable use of smaller boosters—with the goal of simultaneously driving down cost," Shelton said.

Satellites should be built with greater resiliency before they are launched, said Peter Wegner, director of advanced concepts at Utah State University's Space Dynamics Laboratory.

Systems must be hardened so in the event of an attack they can return to their original state and continue providing necessary capabilities, he said.

International treaties are another way the United States could mitigate a future attack, said Douglas Loverro, deputy assistant secretary of defense for space policy, during his testimony before the SASC in March.

The Defense Department is working with the State Department to establish an international code of conduct for responsible space use, he said. It would include standards for "debris limitation, launch notification, on-orbit monitoring and collision avoidance."

While a set of standards will not necessarily deter all spacefaring countries from irresponsible actions, it will help keep space sustainable, he said.

"I am not so naïve as to believe that a simple set of rules will solve all of the major issues we face—they will not; nor would I expect that they will inhibit those who would try to threaten our use of space," Loverro said. "But commonsense rules that can be embraced by a majority of spacefaring nations will help stem the rise of uncontrollable debris, add demonstrably to spaceflight safety and clearly differentiate those who use space responsibly from those who do not."

"All U.S. military satellites are not equally vulnerable to a Chinese ASAT [anti-satellite weapons] attack."

China's Space Program Does Not Threaten the United States

Jaganath Sankaran

Jaganath Sankaran is a former associate with the Project on Managing the Atom at Harvard University's Belfer Center for Science and International Affairs. In the following viewpoint, Sankaran argues that despite claims to the contrary, China's space technology is insufficient to attack American satellites. This is mostly due to China's weak ability to track satellites in orbit. Additionally, China lacks the infrastructure necessary to launch enough attacks in quick succession; this should allay American fears of a Chinese threat in outer space, Sankaran contends.

As you read, consider the following questions:

1. Why does Sankaran say China's intercontinental ballistic missiles pose no threat to American military satellites?

2. According to the viewpoint, what would China have to do to impact US satellite performance meaningfully?

3. What does Sankaran suggest the United States do to integrate China into the global space community?

In May 2013, the Pentagon suggested that a high altitude Chinese suborbital space launch—claimed to be a scientific mission by China—was in reality the first test of an anti-satellite (ASAT) interceptor that would reach all the way to geosynchronous Earth orbit. Previously, on January 11, 2007, China had successfully launched an ASAT missile against one of its own low Earth orbit (LEO) weather satellites.

These and other Chinese actions have provoked strong concerns within the U.S. about China's motivations. James R. Clapper, the U.S. director of national intelligence, for example, recently told a Senate hearing that: "Chinese and Russian military leaders understand the unique information advantages afforded by space systems and are developing capabilities to disrupt U.S. use of space in conflict. Chinese military writings highlight the need to interfere with, damage, and destroy reconnaissance, navigation, and communication satellites."

While these concerns have some validity, all U.S. military satellites are not equally vulnerable to a Chinese ASAT attack. Furthermore, the benefits from an ASAT attack are limited and would not confer decisive military advantage in every plausible conflict.

Limits of the Possible

The substantial range of orbital altitude—1,000 kilometers [km] to 36,000 kilometers—across which satellites operate from poses a challenge to China's ability to attack U.S. military satellites. U.S. intelligence, surveillance and reconnaissance (ISR) satellites that operate at altitudes less than 1,000 kilometers are theoretically most vulnerable to an ASAT attack by China's intermediate-range ballistic missiles (IRBMs). Although the 2007 Chinese ASAT test demonstrated an intercept of this type, there is no publicly available data on the conditions under which the test occurred. How long was the target satellite tracked? Was it transmitting telemetry data providing its orbital location information? These conditions matter. If the U.S. slightly changed the parameters of a satellite's orbit (for example, its inclination), will China still be able to track, target and intercept the satellite?

Unlike the U.S., China has a very limited satellite tracking capability, most of which is based in its territory and possibly a few ships. A first order technical analysis—assuming China cannot predetermine a point of intercept—suggests it would be extremely difficult for China to successfully execute an ASAT operation without extensive tracking capability. This is due to the difference between the velocity of the target satellite and the ASAT missile. The satellite is traveling at approximately 7.5 km/s [kilometers per second]. In the approximately three minutes of boost available to the missile, the satellite travels a distance of 1,350 km. For a successful intercept, in the same three minutes the ASAT missile will have to travel up to the altitude of the satellite (say 800 km) and, at the same time, compensate for the 1,350 km the satellite traverses using its lateral acceleration forces.

Unlike ISR satellites, GPS [global positioning system] and military communication satellites are completely invulnerable to China's current missile arsenal. Even China's most powerful missiles, its solid-fueled intercontinental ballistic missiles (ICBMs) would not be able to reach an altitude of 20,000 km where GPS satellites operate, much less the 36,000 km where U.S. military communications satellites operate. In order to reach higher orbit satellites, China would have to build new and more powerful ICBMs. Even if China manages to develop such an ICBM, it certainly will not be able to easily proliferate a large number of them without imposing substantial financial strain on itself. Alternatively, China can use its liquid-fueled space launch vehicles.

However, even if Chinese space launch vehicles could reach these higher orbits in time to intercept U.S. satellites, executing a number of these launches in quick succession is close to impossible. Its infrastructure limits such a venture. For example, China launched a total of eight annual space launches to orbits higher than LEO in 2012, nine in 2011, eight in 2010, two in 2009 (with one failure), and four in 2008. In the last five years the two quickest back-to-back launches to orbits higher than LEO occurred with a gap of 15 days. Finally, unlike the ICBMs which can be quickly fired, liquid-fueled space launch vehicles take time to fuel and these preparations are very visible. If the U.S. anticipates and observes China preparing for an ASAT attack, it could destroy the launch vehicles during the preparation stages.

Alternate Platforms and Redundancies

Furthermore, the presence of alternate platforms and built-in redundancies substantially limit the advantages that China can obtain from anti-satellite operations against the U.S. For example, in the case [of] ISR satellites, the U.S. possesses an extensive array of airborne platforms that can duplicate and likely outperform many missions that are also performed by satellites. A few of these airborne platforms are: U-2, E-8C Joint Surveillance and Target Attack Radar System (JSTARS), RC-135 Rivet Joint, EP-3 (Aries II), E-3 Sentry and E-2C Hawkeye. In addition, America possesses a number of UAVs [unmanned aerial vehicles] like the RQ-4 Global Hawk, MQ-1 Predator, MQ-SX, MQ-9 Reaper, MQ-1C Gray Eagle, MQ-5 Hunter, MQ-8 Fire Scout and RQ-7. All recent U.S. military operations have extensively employed these airborne ISR systems. In the 2003 Operation Iraqi Freedom, for example, coalition air forces employed 80 aircraft that flew nearly 1,000 ISR sorties during the initial weeks, collecting 42,000 battlefield images and more than 3,000 hours of full motion video.

They also provided 2,400 hours of SIGINT [signals intelligence] coverage and 1,700 hours of moving target indicator data.

These airborne platforms also have standoff capability and should be able to operate safely outside of China's inland air defense systems in a hypothetical conflict in the 180 kilometer long Taiwan Strait. All of these platforms will be used in a conflict in the Taiwan Strait, raising questions about the unique value of attacking U.S. ISR satellites. Why would China choose to focus on attacking ISR satellites when airborne platforms probably pose a much greater threat and would be easier to attack?

In the case of GPS satellites, the redundancy of the constellation limits what China can achieve. The GPS constellation consists of around 30 satellites in six orbital planes. This orbital arrangement guarantees that the navigation signal of at least four satellites can be received at any time all over the world. To meaningfully impact U.S. performance—for example, force U.S. ships to operate without access to accurate GPS navigation signals in the Taiwan Strait region—China would have to successfully attack and disable at least six GPS satellites. Even if six GPS satellites are destroyed in an elaborate ASAT operation, the degradation in navigation signals lasts only for a period of 95 minutes. What would China gain from 95 minutes of GPS degradation? U.S. ships and aircraft have accurate inertial navigation systems that would still permit them to operate in the region. As for the ability to use GPS-guided bombs, the U.S. could shift to laser-guided bombs. In fact, between Operations Enduring Freedom and Iraqi Freedom, DOD [U.S. Department of Defense] decreased the use of GPS-guided bombs by about 13 percent and increased the use of laser-guided bombs by about 10 percent.

Finally, in the case of communication satellites, a Chinese ASAT operation has its own problem: escalation control. The Naval Telecommunications System (NTS) that would be supporting the U.S. Navy in a conflict is very elaborate. It is comprised of three elements: (1) tactical communications among afloat units around a battle group, (2) long-haul communications between the shore-based forward Naval Communications Stations (NAVCOMSTAs) and forward-deployed afloat units, and (3) strategic communication connecting NAVCOM-STAs with National Command Authorities (NCAs).

The first element consists of tactical communication between close formations (25–30 kilometers) using "line-of-sight" radio. For communication with picket ships and between formed groups (300–500 kilometers) "extended line-of-sight" radio is used. Satellites do not play a major role here.

In contrast, the third element, consisting of strategic communications, is largely dependent on satellites. Therefore, the component of NTS that China would be able to disrupt with its ASATs is strategic communications that would connect the NCA with the forward-deployed battle group. This poses a unique problem. Normally, China should prefer to disable the communication capabilities within the forward-deployed battle group and then negotiate with the NCA to have the battle group withdraw or stand down. However, it can only accomplish the opposite. By using ASATs, China would cut off the forward-deployed battle group from its NCA but not be able to significantly disable the battle group's ability to execute its naval mission. China could hope that such an attack might force the battle group to stand down. However, it will also have to contend with the possibility that the battle group commander would act more rashly in the absence of direct guidance from the NCA, particularly if combat maneuvers have been initiated. Would China be willing to take such risk? Arguably, the risk might not be worth the potential escalation it might trigger.

Policy Recommendations

The various arguments expounded [previously] paint a nuanced picture on American vulnerabilities in space and China's potential to exploit it. Just because the U.S. armed forces use satellites more than any other military does not make these satellites immediate and obvious targets. Convincing the Chinese of this might be the best way to dissuade their anti-satellite activities. There are a number of steps the U.S. can take to do that:

1. The presence of alternate systems gives a large measure of operational security to U.S. forces—enabling them to operate in an environment with degraded satellite services. Such systems should be more effectively integrated into U.S. military operations.

2. The U.S. should demonstrate its ability to use measures like satellite sensor shielding and collision avoidance maneuvers for satellites that would dilute an adversary's ASAT potential.

3. Monitoring mechanisms that provide long warning times and the ability to definitively identify an attacker in real time should be a priority. Examples of these include the ground-based Rapid Attack, Identification, Detection, and Reporting System (RAIDRS), which is used to identify, characterize and geo-locate attacks against U.S. satellites, and the upcoming Geosynchronous Space Situational Awareness (SSA) that would provide a continuous monitoring of satellites.

These military-technical solutions might provide some relief; however, it is important to acknowledge and address legitimate Chinese concerns about U.S. weapons programs, including missile defenses in order to dissuade China. Central to the threat of China's ASAT is the incongruence Beijing perceives between the capabilities of U.S. and PLA [People's Liberation Army] forces. While it may not be politically possible to address all Chinese concerns, engaging and addressing some of them is a sensible way to build a stable and cooperative regime in space.

Such inducements will require more cooperative ventures that integrate China more deeply into the global space community. The U.S. could, for example, make available U.S. data on satellite traffic and collisions that would help China streamline its space operations. Such gestures will demonstrate a modicum of goodwill, which can encourage further cooperation. However, the U.S. has been more forthcoming and willing to ink data-sharing arrangements with allies than with China. Although there may be security reasons behind this preference to engage primarily with allies, it is important to realize that China is the nation that needs to be most induced to contribute to the peaceful development of space operations. Any coherent plan to dissuade and deter China from employing an ASAT attack will also have to include bilateral discussions.

Discussions over possible space arms control will provide opportunities to convince China of important thresholds. For example, as Micah Zenko of the Council of Foreign Relations suggests, if China believes shooting down U.S. early-warning satellites would be de-escalatory and stabilizing in a naval encounter with the U.S., it should be told clearly that is not the case. U.S. military satellites that provide missile early-warning have a tactical utility but, more importantly, they also serve to maintain the stability of nuclear deterrence between the U.S. and China. China should be convinced that attacking these satellites will provoke swift reprisal attacks. Finally, engaging in negotiations over space security and demonstrating leadership with such measures will help characterize the U.S. as a responsible actor, and therefore render it with the authority to respond with force when an attack is made on its own or allied space assets.

Periodical and Internet Sources Bibliography

The following articles have been selected to supplement the diverse views presented in this chapter.

Lee Billings	"The Shifting Politics of NASA's Astronaut Program," *Scientific American*, February 27, 2015.
R.D. Boozer	"Allow NASA to Do Great Things Again," Space.com, December 9, 2013.
Chris Carberry	"The Enigma of Presidential 'Space' Politics," *Space Review*, December 1, 2014.
Stephen Clark	"Europe, China Issue Call for Joint Science Mission," Spaceflight Now, January 24, 2015.
Wilson Dizard	"The Year in Space: Politics Could Steer Space Explorers in 2015," Al Jazeera, December 25, 2014.
Jeffrey Kluger	"The Silly Reason the Chinese Aren't Allowed on the Space Station," *Time*, May 29, 2015.
Katherine Mangu-Ward	"Is the Ocean the Real Final Frontier?," *Slate*, September 4, 2013.
Michele Penna	"China Mulls Building New Solar Power Station . . . in Space," Asian Correspondent, April 3, 2015.
Mark Strauss	"Should We Be Exploring the Oceans Instead of Space?," *io9*, August 11, 2014.
David Tweed	"New Report Finds China's Space Plans Threaten U.S. Military Ability," Bloomberg Business, March 2, 2015.
Brian Wu	"Future of Spaceflight Could Rest in the Hands of the Private Sector," Science Times, May 7, 2015.

OPPOSING
VIEWPOINTS®
SERIES

CHAPTER 4

What Is the Science Behind Space Exploration?

Chapter Preface

Since the infancy of space exploration in the 1950s, people have continually worked to improve and modernize the technology required to launch objects and people into outer space. These improvements are meant both to increase the efficiency of spacecraft, making them last longer while doing more, and to reduce the costs of space missions, which tend to run into the billions of dollars.

One area of space technology that scientists in the early twenty-first century continue to study is rocket fuel—specifically, what new, safer, more inexpensive types of fuel can be used to propel spacecraft into Earth's orbit and the far reaches of space. The most commonly used type of rocket fuel since the 1950s is chemical propulsion. This generally involves the mixing of liquid oxygen with liquid hydrogen, each of which is stored in its own tank in the rocket at extremely cold temperatures until they are mixed and ignited. The sudden, extreme heat of about six thousand degrees Fahrenheit turns the liquids into gases, which burn so strongly that they propel the rocket and its attached spacecraft out of Earth's atmosphere and into space.

While chemical-propulsion rockets are constructed and operated as safely as they can be, the mixing and combusting of these two highly volatile elements has always made liftoff and flight subject to possible accident. A notable such incident occurred in 1986 soon after the liftoff of the space shuttle *Challenger*, which exploded and disintegrated after rocket gases escaped the motor chamber. Therefore, in the twenty-first century, some scientists advocate for safer fuel alternatives such as electrical propulsion, which opponents reject as safe but weak, and nuclear propulsion, which many consider efficient but dangerous. In 2010, amid this continuing research into the perfect rocket fuel, British aerospace engineer Robert

Shawyer invented the EM Drive, an electromagnetic rocket-propulsion system boasting thrust without propellant. This claim quickly earned the drive comparison to the fabled warp drives of science fiction that are capable of infinitely powering spacecraft to all corners of the universe faster than the speed of light. Shawyer asserted that bouncing electromagnetic microwaves around the inside of a rocket-propulsion system would convert electrical energy into enough thrust to lift a spacecraft into orbit—all without expelling any propellant whatsoever. In addition to generating sustainable fuel for interstellar travel, the drive would also eliminate the risk of rocket explosions—and, consequently, astronaut deaths—during flight.

While the National Aeronautics and Space Administration (NASA) and other world space agencies studied and tested their own versions of the EM Drive in the mid-2010s, the device was summarily dismissed by scientists, who claimed its purported technology violated the laws of physics and was therefore impossible. They cited Isaac Newton's third law of physics: that every action will cause an equal and opposite reaction. If the drive operated as Shawyer proposed it would, opponents claimed, it would produce more energy than was put into it. This would also violate the law of conservation of energy, they said, which states that energy could not be created or destroyed in a closed system. Despite these claims, NASA reported in 2015 that it had tested an electromagnetic drive in a vacuum and determined that it had in fact produced a weak amount of thrust. Soon after the test, however, NASA stated explicitly that its experiments with the drive had yielded no tangible results and that the public should not expect rocket warp drives to appear in the near future.

The following chapter presents viewpoints that explore the scientific aspects of contemporary and developing space exploration technology. Subjects covered include nuclear rocket fuel, human hibernation in space, the possibility of life else-where in the universe, and the practical potential of 3-D print-ing.

> *"Nuclear propulsion represents the next inevitable phase of rocket technology for space exploration."*

Nuclear Power Is the Spacecraft Fuel of the Future

Rob Eubank

Rob Eubank is a writer for Penny4NASA. In the following viewpoint, Eubank argues that nuclear energy should be used to fuel all future spacecraft. This fuel is simpler to use and more efficient than all previous alternatives, he believes. Additionally, by its design, Eubank writes, it is also extremely safe and would be unlikely ever to cause a nuclear explosion, making the prospect more attractive.

As you read, consider the following questions:

1. What two types of rocket propulsions does Eubank say are inefficient, and why?

2. What does Eubank say is the benefit of solid-core nuclear thermal rockets?

3. What does Eubank say is the only concern with using nuclear-powered craft in suborbital space?

To achieve any measure of space travel there is one tool that has always been indispensable, rockets. Rockets have been the primary tool for sending spacecraft into orbit and accelerating them beyond Earth orbit to other planets in the solar system, and for a few craft, on their way out to the rest of the galaxy.

Despite the amazing advances in rocket technology since the days of Apollo, NASA [National Aeronautics and Space Administration] still is forced to rely on chemical combustion to propel vehicles off Earth and to space destinations in a relatively short time period. Chemical rocket engines, while producing a lot of thrust, are highly inefficient and very dangerous, as several rocket accidents in the past have proven. Electrical propulsion is a useful alternative for long-term small probes due to its high efficiency, but it produces very low thrust and is not useful for shorter-term manned missions.

Many theoretical concepts for high efficiency and high thrust propulsion offer a tantalizing view for how space travel in the future might work, but for now such concepts are technically unfeasible. There is, however, an option in between the future and now that uses existing technology. The best part is, it is an old idea.

Reactor Power

Nuclear thermal rockets, or NTRs for short, are rocket engines that utilize a nuclear fission reactor to heat propellant instead of igniting combustible propellants. The advantages include much higher specific impulses due to a higher range of exhaust velocities that chemical rockets can't achieve due to limits of the combustible fuels. The idea is surprisingly simple: take a nuclear reactor like the ones used for power generation today, but instead of using it to heat water into steam for power turbines, heat propellant instead and run it out of a rocket nozzle for thrust. This is the simplest form of NTR, which is called a solid-core NTR. In fact, it is so simple it has already been done, just not in space.

In 1955, the Atomic Energy Commission [AEC] started Project Rover, aimed at the development of engines utilizing nuclear technologies, which were in their prime in the 1950s in America. Four basic designs came from this and 20 rockets were tested, but the AEC work was intended to study the reactor design itself for rocket use, rather than actually build a rocket. In 1961, NASA began the Nuclear Engine for Rocket Vehicle Application program, or NERVA for short, to formalize the entry of nuclear thermal engines into space exploration. In fact, it was President [John F.] Kennedy's hope that Project Rover and the NERVA program would be the next step after Apollo, stating such in his famous speech to a joint session of Congress establishing the goal of landing a man on the moon.

Directly comparing the performance of two different rocket systems is not simple however. There are ways in which chemical propulsion is better than nuclear and vice versa. The most basic form of solid-core NTR provides much better specific impulse, a measure of how efficient a rocket is (think gas mileage), but doesn't have comparable thrust. It also takes a lot of time to warm up a nuclear rocket and cool it down between firings, putting stress on the system. The best way around this is what is called a bimodal NTR, which uses the reactor to both provide rocket thrust and supply power to the spacecraft at the same time. The reactor is started up once and when rocket firings are done it is cooled down to regular operating levels and a Brayton power conversion system is used to supply the spacecraft with power. This employs a different working fluid through a turbine and a radiator to cool it. Thus the reactor only needs to be started up and shut off once per mission.

An even better option is the trimodal NTR conceptualized by Pratt & Whitney [an American aerospace manufacturer]. This takes the bimodal concept and adds another NTR concept referred to as LANTR, or LOX-augmented NTR, to make the Triton engine. The LANTR mode allows for more thrust by injecting liquid oxygen into the nozzle to act as an afterburner. This design then allows for a ship to have high thrust, high specific impulse, or power generation from one engine depending on the setting.

There are even more ambitious ideas for NTRs, including liquid core and gas core engines, but they have never been built beyond the conceptual stage and present several new challenges, among which is a high tendency of releasing radioactive elements into the exhaust. Solid-core NTRs keep the radioactive elements away from the propellant, thus making them safer. However, all solid-core tests such as NERVA resulted in engines with a thrust-to-weight ratio lower than one, meaning it could not lift a rocket off Earth.

This leads to the obvious fact that despite Kennedy's high hopes and NASA's research, nuclear engines never did get used for actual spacecraft. There is a complicated set of reasons for this, including cost factor, various issues and most importantly public opinion. The growing public dissatisfaction with nuclear weapons and nuclear power by proxy as a result of the Cold War [nonviolent post–World War II conflict between the United States and the Soviet Union] arms race and later accidents like Chernobyl [the site of a catastrophic nuclear power plant disaster in Ukraine] made it a lot less likely that people would like the idea of a nuclear-powered rocket flying, even if it could be safe. Today, nuclear weapon treaties forbid nuclear weapons in space, thus making ideas like Project Orion, which used full nuclear bombs for propulsion, infeasible. Such treaties do not disallow nuclear reactors like what NERVA used, however.

Nuclear-Powered Rockets to Mars

NASA chiefs have said that sending a manned mission to Mars is 'necessary if the human race is to survive'.

But the huge amounts of chemical rocket fuel needed to complete such a mission would require deep pockets—the launch costs alone would be more than $12 billion (£7 billion).

Added to this is the time it takes. The space agency estimates that a round-trip human expedition to Mars would take more than four years using current technology.

Rocket-powered fusion, however, could one day allow 30- and 90-day expeditions to Mars by making the trip more practical and less costly, experts claim.

Scientists envision using a nuclear reactor to heat hydrogen to very high temperatures, which will then expand through a spacecraft's nozzle to generate thrust.

Recent advances in manipulating nuclear fusion could mean that astronauts are now a step closer to our nearest planetary neighbour.

'Using existing rocket fuels, it's nearly impossible for humans to explore much beyond Earth' said lead researcher John Slough. . . .

[Slough said,] 'We hope we can interest the world with the fact that fusion isn't always 40 years away and doesn't always cost $2 billion.'

Ellie Zolfagharifard,
"Could We Travel to Mars in 30 Days?
NASA Believes Nuclear-Powered Rockets Could Make
Trip Faster and Cheaper," Daily Mail, *April 25, 2014.*

Challenges and the Future

NASA has always wanted their vehicles to be safe and not cause harm to anyone. As such, the biggest issue with these engines is radiation. Fears of radioactive material dispersed into the atmosphere, or a nuclear explosion happening, are common. However, despite the horrible accidents that have plagued nuclear reactors before, they are more safe than many realize and ... can be done so that no radioactive material leaves the nozzle. A nuclear explosion is highly unlikely since reactors are not designed to act like nuclear bombs and are more controlled. This aside though, the simplest option is to not use them in the atmosphere at all and make nuclear engines only for use in space, while using chemical engines to get to orbit. The only worry is a suborbital structural failure, but designs for the reactors are very robust, leaving it unlikely for radioactive material to be spread. As for fears of the reactor irradiating astronauts, there are ways of shielding them, but studies have shown that the shorter travel times NTRs allow result in less radiation exposure by passengers due to them spending less time in space exposed to cosmic radiation.

Continued research is still being done; in the 1970s a small nuclear engine was designed for possible use with the space shuttle in place of the space shuttle main engines [SSME]. The design provided a theoretical specific impulse of 975 seconds, much greater than the 363–452 seconds of the SSME for only slightly less of the SSME mass fraction. It was clearly not chosen for the space shuttle however. Continued research under Project Timberwind as part of the Strategic Defense Initiative was done between 1987 and 1991, and in 2012 Icarus Interstellar and General Propulsion Sciences began a development project known as Project Bifrost to develop an NTR system for interplanetary missions.

While it hasn't been used yet despite all the research behind it, nuclear propulsion represents the next inevitable phase of rocket technology for space exploration and it can help humanity to unlock the solar system. With more research and funding, NASA can help to improve this technology and make it safer. If you think NASA should continue to develop new innovative propulsion technologies like this, let Congress know.

> "Accidents involving nuclear-powered space devices have happened with substantial amounts of radioactive particles released on Earth."

Nuclear Power in Space Is Dangerous

Karl Grossman

Karl Grossman is a writer for the news organization Nation of Change. In the following viewpoint, Grossman contends that nuclear fuel should not be used to power spacecraft, as this risks accidents that could prove catastrophic for people on Earth. Such an accident, he writes, could have the same effect as the detonation of a nuclear bomb. Grossman instead praises the benefits of solar energy for spacecraft fuel.

As you read, consider the following questions:

1. What historical incident does Grossman cite as evidence that nuclear reactors in space can still cause harm on Earth?

2. What does Grossman say would be the breakdown of the cost of decontamination on Earth after a nuclear spacecraft accident?

3. What other fuel alternative for spacecraft does Grossman say was proposed at a Starship Congress?

The recent crash of Virgin Galactic's SpaceShipTwo and explosion on launch three days earlier of an Antares rocket further underline the dangers of inserting nuclear material in the always perilous spaceflight equation as the U.S. and Russia still plan.

"SpaceShipTwo has experienced an in-flight anomaly," Virgin Galactic tweeted after the spacecraft, on which $500 million has been spent for development, exploded on October 31 [2014] after being released by its mother ship. One pilot [Michael Alsbury] was killed, another [Peter Siebold] seriously injured. Richard Branson, Virgin Galactic founder, hoped to begin flying passengers on SpaceShipTwo this spring. Some 800 people, including actor Leonard DiCaprio and physicist Stephen Hawking, have signed up for $250,000-a person tickets to take a suborbital ride. SpaceShipTwo debris was spread over the Mojave Desert in California.

Three days before, on Wallops Island, Virginia, an Antares rocket operated by Orbital Sciences Corp. blew up seconds after launch. It was carrying 5,000 pounds of supplies and experiments to the International Space Station. The cost of the rocket alone was put at $200 million. NASA [National Aeronautics and Space Administration], in a statement, said that the rocket "suffered a catastrophic anomaly." The word anomaly, defined as something that deviates from what is standard, normal or expected, has for years been a space program euphemism for a disastrous accident.

"These two recent space 'anomalies' remind us that technology frequently goes wrong," said Bruce Gagnon, coordinator of the Global Network Against Weapons and Nuclear

Power in Space. "When you consider adding nuclear power into the mix it becomes an explosive combination. We've long been sounding the alarm that nuclear power in space is not something the public nor the planet can afford to take a chance on."

But "adding nuclear power into the mix" is exactly what the U.S. and Russia are planning. Both countries have been using nuclear power on space missions for decades and accidents involving their nuclear-powered space devices have happened, with substantial amounts of radioactive particles released on Earth.

Now, a major expansion in space nuclear power activity is planned, with the development by both nations of nuclear-powered rockets for trips to Mars.

Nuclear Popularity

One big U.S. site for this is NASA's Marshall Space Flight Center in Huntsville, Alabama. "NASA Researchers Studying Advanced Nuclear Rocket Technologies," announced NASA last year. At the center, it said, "The Nuclear Cryogenic Propulsion [Stage] team is tackling a three-year project to demonstrate the viability of nuclear propulsion technologies." In them, a "nuclear rocket uses a nuclear reactor to heat hydrogen to very high temperatures, which expands through a nozzle to generate thrust. Nuclear rocket engines generate higher thrust and are more than twice as efficient as conventional chemical engines."

"A first-generation nuclear cryogenic propulsion system could propel human explorers to Mars more efficiently than conventional spacecraft, reducing crew's exposure to harmful space radiation and other effects of long-term space missions," NASA went on. "It could also transport heavy cargo and science payloads."

And out at Los Alamos National Laboratory, the DUFF project, for Demonstration Using Flattop Fission, is moving ahead to develop a "robust fission reactor prototype that could be used as a power system for space travel," according to *TechNewsWorld*. The laboratory's Advanced Nuclear Technology Division is running the joint Department of Energy–NASA project. "Nuclear Power Could Blast Humans into Deep Space" was the headline of *TechNewsWorld*'s 2012 article about it. It quoted Dr. Michael Gruntman, professor of aerospace engineering and systems architecture at the University of Southern California, saying, "If we want solar system exploration, we must utilize nuclear technology." The article declared: "Without the risk, there will be no reward."

And in Texas, near NASA's Johnson Space Center, the Ad Astra Rocket Company of former U.S. astronaut Franklin Chang Díaz is busy working on what it calls the Variable Specific Impulse Magnetoplasma Rocket or VASIMR. Chang Díaz began Ad Astra after retiring from NASA in 2005. He's its president and CEO [chief executive officer]. The VASIMR system could utilize solar power, related *SpaceNews* last year, but "using a VASIMR engine to make a superfast Mars run would require incorporating a nuclear reactor that cranks out megawatts of power, Chang Díaz said, adding that developing this type of powerful reactor should be high on the nation's to-do list." Chang Díaz told Voice of America that by using a nuclear reactor for power "we could do a mission to Mars that would take about 39 days, one-way." NASA director Charles Bolden, also a former astronaut as well as a Marine Corps major general, has been a booster of Ad Astra's project.

Ad Astra and the Nuclear Cryogenic Propulsion project have said their designs would include nuclear systems only starting up when "out of the atmosphere" to prevent, in the event of an accident, "spreading radiation back to Earth."

However, this isn't a fail-safe plan. The Soviet Union followed this practice on the satellites powered by nuclear reactors that it launched between the 1960s and 1980s. This included the Kosmos 954. Its onboard reactor was only allowed to go critical after it was in orbit, but it subsequently came crashing back to Earth in 1978, breaking up and spreading radioactive debris on the Northwest Territories of Canada.

As to Russia now, "A groundbreaking Russian nuclear space travel propulsion system will be ready by 2017 and will power a ship capable of long-haul interplanetary missions by 2025, giving Russia a head start in the outer-space race," the Russian news agency RT reported in 2012. "Nuclear power has generally been considered a valid alternative to fossil fuels to power spacecraft, as it is the only energy source capable of producing the enormous thrust needed for interplanetary travel. . . . The revolutionary propulsion system falls in line with recently announced plans for Russia to conquer space. . . . Entitled Space Development Strategies up to 2030, Russia aims to send probes to Mars, Jupiter, and Venus, as well as establish a series of bases on the moon."

This year OSNet Daily, in an article headlined "Russia Advances Development of Nuclear Powered Spacecraft," reported that in 2013 work on the Russian nuclear rocket moved "to the design stage."

As for space probes, many U.S. and Russian probes have until recently gotten their onboard electrical power from systems fueled with plutonium hotly radioactive from the start.

Also, the U.S. has begun to power Mars rovers with plutonium. After using solar power on Mars rovers, in 2012 NASA launched a Mars rover it named Curiosity fueled with 10.6 pounds of plutonium. NASA plans to launch a Mars rover nearly identical to Curiosity, which it is calling Mars 2020, in 2020.

Accidents and Alternatives

As devastating in terms of financial damage were last week's explosions of the Virgin Galactic SpaceShipTwo and Antares rocket, an accident involving a nuclear-powered vehicle or device could be far more costly.

The NASA Final Environmental Impact Statement [EIS] for the Curiosity (then called Mars Science Laboratory) mission states, for example, that the cost of decontamination of areas affected by dispersed plutonium would be $267 million for each square mile of farmland, $478 million for each square mile of forests and $1.5 billion for each square mile of "mixed-use urban areas."

Odds of an accident were acknowledged as being low. The EIS said a launch accident discharging plutonium had a 1-in-420 chance of happening and could "release material into the regional area defined . . . within . . . 62 miles of the launch pad" on Cape Canaveral, Florida. The EIS said that "overall" on the mission, the likelihood of plutonium being released was 1-in-220. If there were an accident resulting in plutonium fallout that occurred before the rocket carrying Curiosity broke through Earth's gravitational field, people could be affected in a broad swath of Earth "anywhere between 28-degrees north and 28-degrees south latitude" on Earth, said the EIS.

Gagnon said at the time: "NASA sadly appears committed to maintaining its dangerous alliance with the nuclear industry. . . . The taxpayers are being asked once again to pay for nuclear missions that could endanger the lives of all the people on the planet. Have we not learned anything from Chernobyl [the site of a catastrophic nuclear power plant disaster in Ukraine in 1986] and Fukushima [the site of a nuclear disaster caused by a tsunami following an earthquake in Japan in 2011]? We don't need to be launching nukes into space. It's not a gamble we can afford to take."

Curiosity made it up, and to Mars.

But in NASA's history of nuclear power shots, happening since the 1950s, there have been accidents. The worst among the 26 U.S. space nuclear missions listed in the Curiosity EIS occurred in 1964 and involved the SNAP-9A [Systems for Nuclear Auxiliary Power] plutonium system aboard a satellite that failed to achieve orbit and dropped to Earth, disintegrating as it fell. Its plutonium fuel dispersed widely. That accident spurred NASA to develop solar energy for satellites and now all satellites are solar powered as is the International Space Station.

And in recent times, solar power has been increasingly shown to be practical even to generate onboard electricity for missions far out in space. On its way to Jupiter now is NASA's Juno space probe, chemically propelled and with solar photovoltaic panels generating all its onboard electricity. When Juno reaches Jupiter in 2016 it will be nearly 500 million miles from the sun, but the high-efficiency solar cells will still be generating power.

In August, the European Space Agency's Rosetta space probe, similarly solar powered, rendezvoused with a comet in deep space, 400 million miles from Earth.

Advances, too, have been made in propelling spacecraft in the vacuum of space. The Japan Aerospace Exploration Agency in 2010 launched what it termed a "space yacht" it called IK-AROS [Interplanetary Kite-craft Accelerated by Radiation of the Sun] which successfully got its propulsion power from the pressure on its large sails of ionizing particles emitted by the sun.

Among other ways of propelling spacecraft, discussed at a Starship Congress last year in Texas, was a system using orbiting lasers to direct beams onto a spacecraft. The magazine *New Scientist* said, "beam sails are regarded as the most promising tech for a starship."

A scientist long involved in laser space power research is Geoff Landis of the Photovoltaics and Space Environment Branch at NASA's Glenn Research Center in Cleveland who, in a 2002 NASA publication, "The Edge of Sunshine," wrote: "In the long term, solar arrays will not have to rely on the sun. We're investigating the concept of using lasers to beam photons to solar arrays. If you make a powerful enough laser and can aim the beam, there really isn't any edge of sunshine with a big enough lens, we could beam light to a space probe half-way to Alpha Centauri [closest star system to the solar system]!"

> "We must be prepared to find life where
> we don't expect it and in forms we have
> never seen before."

Life Could Exist Elsewhere in the Universe

Stephen Morgan

Stephen Morgan is editor at large for Digital Journal. *In the following viewpoint, Morgan contends that the traditional wisdom of extraterrestrial life existing only under conditions similar to Earth's is not necessarily true. As evidence, he points to some "extremophile" species on Earth, including, for example, forms of bacteria that can survive intense levels of otherwise harmful radiation. For this reason, Morgan believes, life could exist on numerous, non-earthlike planets.*

As you read, consider the following questions:

1. According to the viewpoint, under what harsh conditions do *Aquifex* bacteria live?

2. What does Morgan say is surprising about the way endoliths live?

3. According to Morgan, what change is being proposed to the Planetary Habitability Index?

A group of scientists is proposing that alien life-forms may not need conditions similar to Earth to survive and that we should not exclude the possibility of other "exotic" types of life existing in the universe.

It seems that we must be prepared to find life where we don't expect it and in forms we have never seen before and this could even be the case within our own solar system!

An article in yesterday's [November 16, 2014] Space.com says a group of scientists, who published a paper in the journal *Life*, believes that we may be too "Earth-centric" in our search for life and we may be limiting ourselves in our concept of what life is and how it can develop.

Extreme Life-Forms

Most exploration of the cosmos has so far centred on finding planets with the same environment as our own. It is possible we will find extraterrestrial life that needs neither oxygen, water nor sunlight to survive. Even on our own planet, we have discovered bizarre life-forms living in conditions which defy our standard definitions of nature.

An article in Live Science gives some examples of extreme life-forms or "extremophiles" here on Earth which contradict existing biological theories. We know, for instance, that some bacteria can live inside rocks and certain microbes can withstand severe levels of radiation and temperature.

The *Aquifex* bacteria, for example, live in hot springs in Yellowstone National Park at temperatures of more [than] 205°F or 90°C. Then, there are *Thermococcus* microbes living in the thermal vents of underwater volcanoes at super-high temperatures and using so little energy to survive through chemical reactions thought impossible. At the other extreme, there are psychrophiles which can exist in super-low temperatures in ice, glaciers and deep oceans.

Even more strange are *Deinococcus radiodurans* bacteria which are immune to 15,000 gray doses of radiation, while 10 grays would kill a human. Endoliths live so deep underground that there is virtually no water and scientists believe they may survive by living on iron, potassium and sulphur, while newly discovered Loriciferans survive without oxygen at all!

The group of scientists who is suggesting the existence of such life in outer space says that creatures could exist without water and still evolve and survive on CO_2 alone or what they call "supercritical" carbon dioxide, which has the properties of both a liquid and a gas. While CO_2 chemical reactions aren't considered capable of creating conditions for life as we know it, supercritical CO_2 could create more stable conditions for enzymes than water does.

Scientists have studied supercritical CO_2 in the lab and have now found that certain bacteria are tolerant of it and some microbes are present within it. Supercritical CO_2 is known to exist in our oceans, but at depths which are impossible to explore.

The researchers believe other worlds may be based on supercritical CO_2 and exotic forms of life could exist there. Indeed, they even hypothesize that this might be the case on nearby Venus, which in an earlier period in its existence had conditions similar to Earth, and it is possible that remnants of this life have survived in the current CO_2 environment.

Air & Space magazine explains, "Carbon dioxide is usually not considered a suitable solvent for life, at least not on Earth. But its chemical and physical properties change quite dramatically when it becomes supercritical. Above its critical point, CO_2 mixes well with a variety of organic compounds. It participates in a number of organic synthesis reactions, and some bacteria and their enzymes have been shown to be active with supercritical CO_2 as a solvent."

Life May Exist on Europa

Imagine the bottom of an ocean. The water is icy cold and impenetrably dark, without even a glimmer of sunlight. But in one patch of the ocean floor, a jet of hot water spurts upward out of a rocky vent. This water is laced with life-giving chemicals, and around it a collection of strange microorganisms has gathered.

These tiny organisms are like nothing anyone has ever seen before. But that's no surprise, because we're not on Earth. We're 630 million km [kilometers] from Earth, on Europa, one of the moons of Jupiter.

Or at least, we could be. Europa is one of the few places in our solar system where life could exist. It's believed to have an ocean up to 100 km deep, ten times as deep as any ocean on Earth, which could contain twice as much water as our entire planet. All the conditions for life may be met, somewhere in those dark waters.

So far we haven't looked, so we don't know if anything is alive down there. But there are clues to be found much closer to home, in an environment that's almost as extreme.

Deep under the thick ice of Antarctica, there are hundreds of hidden lakes. Some of them have been isolated for millions of years. But in the last few years, scientists have started to explore them, in the hope of finding life.

Antarctica's lakes are the best analogue we have for Europa's hidden ocean. So if life can endure the conditions under the Antarctic ice, the odds of finding it on Europa will improve. What's more, knowing how life survives in these hidden lakes will tell scientists what to look for when they seek it on other worlds.

Melissa Hogenboom,
"Europa May Be Home to Alien Life,"
BBC, March 26, 2015.

Broader Habitability

An article in Wired.com quotes physicist Abel Méndez of the University of Puerto Rico, home to the giant Arecibo telescope used to scour the universe for signs of life. "We are trying not to be geocentric, calculating planetary habitability independent of liquid water," he said.

Abel Méndez's team is proposing to rank planets by two scales rather than one. It suggests that a new broader Planetary Habitability Index (PHI) should be added to the current Earth Similarity Index (ESI) which is being used now, Wired.com explains.

"The first index looks at how close a planet is to Earth in mass, temperature, and composition while the second is based on whether or not it possesses more exotic chemistries, liquids, and energy sources than found on our planet. *Alien life could be based on elements other than carbon, require liquids other than water, and gain energy through means other than sunlight.*"

Within our own solar system, for instance, Saturn's moon Titan is a tiny world where water is only available in frozen chunks hard as rock. But its temperature range makes possible the existence of lakes and rivers of liquid hydrocarbons, leading some researchers to speculate that native life could exist there.

Scientists have discovered more than 700 planets outside our solar system, most of which have been written off as candidates for life because of their orbits or gas-based character. However, the current research would now include them as possible habitats for exotic life-forms completely unrelated to us.

> *"In addition to cutting down on the need for room and supplies, keeping crews in hibernation would also save on another all-important factor: costs."*

Human Hibernation Could Benefit Space Travel

Matt Williams

Matt Williams is a writer who has contributed to Universe Today.com. In the following viewpoint, Williams argues that human hibernation could significantly benefit future manned space missions. He says that the National Aeronautics and Space Administration (NASA) is considering hibernation as a way for astronauts to enter a state of deep sleep at the beginning of their mission and then wake up near the end, arriving at their deep-space destination rested instead of taxed from the long journey. Additionally, Williams says having astronauts asleep during long journeys could reduce the size of the spacecraft and the amount of food needed, which would save money.

As you read, consider the following questions:

1. What technology does Williams suggest using to induce human hibernation in space?

2. According to the viewpoint, how does SpaceWorks suggest hibernating astronauts will be kept healthy on their long transits?

3. What psychological benefit does Williams say hibernation would provide to astronauts?

Manned missions to deep space present numerous challenges. In addition to the sheer amount of food, water and air necessary to keep a crew alive for months (or years) at a time, there's also the question of keeping them busy for the entirety of a long-duration flight. Exercise is certainly an option, but the necessary equipment will take up space and be a drain on power.

In addition, they'll need room to move around, places to sleep, eat, work, and relax during their down time. Otherwise, they will be at risk of succumbing to feelings of claustrophobia, anxiety, insomnia, and depression—among other things.

The Deep Sleep

NASA [National Aeronautics and Space Administration] has been looking at a few options, and one proposed solution is to put these crews into an induced state of hypothermia resulting in torpor—a kind of hibernation. Rather than being awake for months or years on end, astronauts could enter a state of deep sleep at the beginning of their mission and then wake up near the end. This way, they would arrive refreshed and ready to work, rather than haggard and maybe even insane.

If this is starting to sound familiar, it's probably because the concept has been explored extensively by science fiction. Though it goes by different names—cryosleep, reefersleep, cryostasis, etc.—the notion of space explorers preserving their bodies through cryogenic suspension has been touched upon by numerous sci-fi authors, movies, and franchises.

But NASA's plan is a little different than what you might remember from *2001: A Space Odyssey* or *Aliens*. Instead of astronauts stepping into a tube and having their temperature lowered, torpor would be induced via the RhinoChill—a device that uses invasive tubes to shoot cooling liquid up the nose and into the base of the brain.

To research the technology, NASA has teamed up with SpaceWorks [Enterprises, Inc.], an Atlanta-based aerospace company that is investigating procedures for putting space crews into hibernation. During this year's International Astronautical Congress—which took place from Sept. 29th to Oct. 3rd [2014] in Toronto—representatives from SpaceWorks shared their vision.

According to the company, inducing torpor in a crew of astronauts would eliminate the need for accommodations like galleys, exercise equipment, and large living quarters. Instead, robots could electrically stimulate key muscle groups and intravenously deliver sustenance to ensure the health and well-being of the astronauts while in transit.

As Dr. [John E.] Bradford, president of SpaceWorks Enterprises Inc., told Universe Today via email:

"We have completed the initial evaluation of our concept which demonstrated significant benefits against non-torpor Mars mission approaches and established the medical plausibility of torpor. We have expanded our team and put together a development plan that we are in the process of executing. While the longer-term goal of enabling access to Mars is our ultimate objective, we have a number of near-term, commercial applications for this technology that we will develop along the way."

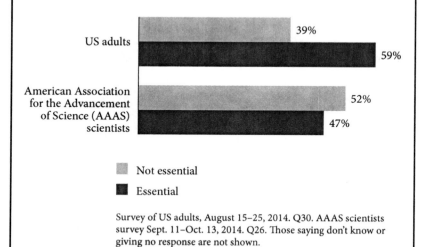

US Space Program and Human Astronauts

Percentage of each group saying it is essential or not essential to include the use of human astronauts in the future of the US space program.

US adults
39%
59%

American Association
for the Advancement
of Science (AAAS)
scientists
52%
47%

▢ Not essential
■ Essential

Survey of US adults, August 15–25, 2014. Q30. AAAS scientists survey Sept. 11–Oct. 13, 2014. Q26. Those saying don't know or giving no response are not shown.

TAKEN FROM: Cary Funk and Lee Rainie, "Chapter 3: Attitudes and Beliefs on Science and Technology Topics," *Public and Scientists' Views on Science and Society*, Pew Research Center, January 29, 2015.

Savings and Benefits

In addition to cutting down on the need for room and supplies, keeping crews in hibernation would also save on another all-important factor: costs. With a crew in stasis, ships could be built smaller or have more room to accommodate safety features like radiation shields. At the same time, smaller, lighter ships would mean that material, construction, and fuel costs would be lower.

According to SpaceWorks' mockups, the size of a crew's living quarters for a Mars mission could be reduced from the currently proposed dimensions of 8.2x9 meters to just 4.3x7.5. Also, current projections indicate that a Mars ready-habitat for a 4-person crew would weigh roughly 31 tons. But the company claims that a torpor-stasis habitat could weigh as little as 15.

Of course, SpaceWorks also emphasized the psychological benefits. Rather than being awake for the entire 180-day journey, the crew would be able to go to sleep and wake up upon arrival. This would ensure that no one succumbs to "madness" during the months-long journey and does something terrible—like take their own life or those of the crew!

Naturally, there is still plenty of research and development that needs to be done before a torpor hibernation system can be considered a feasible option for space travel. RhinoChill has so far only been used in therapeutic scenarios here on Earth. The next step will be to test it in orbit.

Luckily, the potential savings during a trip to Mars or somewhere in the outer solar system could be just the incentive to make it happen. And no matter what, it seems that some form of induced hibernation will be necessary if ever humanity is to explore the depths of space.

"We are at the dawn of a new era in space and my company is excited to be working at the forefront," Bradford said. "I believe our technology will be required to support human missions to Mars. It offers an affordable solution by leveraging ongoing medical research to address challenges spanning engineering, human health, and psychology for which we do not have alternate solutions. This can be ready for the first Mars mission, and we are talking with partners to make this happen."

"There's still a considerable amount of time and research that needs to happen before we send astronauts off to Mars via the shores of sleep."

Human Hibernation Can Benefit Space Travel but Presents Numerous Challenges

Mary Beth Griggs

Mary Beth Griggs is a science journalist. In the following viewpoint, Griggs argues that although induced human hibernation could benefit astronauts on interplanetary missions, the technology requires more research before it can be considered foolproof. She states the dangers of using hibernation include possible impaired brain function as well as loss of muscle and bone density. If these issues and more could be researched and solved, Griggs believes, human hibernation would pose an excellent solution to long human spaceflights.

As you read, consider the following questions:

1. What kind of drop in body temperature does Griggs say would be sufficient to induce human hibernation?

2. What does Griggs say is one of the main issues opposing the use of therapeutic hypothermia in space?

3. What is the problem of intracranial pressure that astronauts sometimes face?

NASA [National Aeronautics and Space Administration] wants to know whether it's really possible to put astronauts into 'suspended animation' for long-distance space travel.

The first astronauts who head off to Mars might make the entire 180-day journey while they're fast asleep. In a NASA-commissioned study on human stasis, aerospace engineers at SpaceWorks [Enterprises, Inc.] have found that the benefits of placing a crew in suspended animation for the duration of the journey could be legion. Without living spaces or kitchen facilities, the ship carrying the crew could be lighter and smaller. With everyone basically in hibernation, with a lower metabolic rate, future missions can reduce consumables like food and water by up to 70 percent. And having an unconscious crew also reduces the grueling boredom and chances of personality clashes before humanity can complete the small step/ giant leap onto the red planet.

Studies and Trials

It sounds practically perfect in every way, but there's still a considerable amount of time and research that needs to happen before we send astronauts off to Mars via the shores of sleep. The technology that SpaceWorks is looking at is a form of therapeutic hypothermia that will drop the temperature of the astronauts' bodies by just 5 to 10 degrees Fahrenheit, reducing their metabolism and putting them in a kind of hibernation. "It doesn't take much to get the body to start slowing down," says John [E.] Bradford, president of SpaceWorks Enterprises.

Though it involves chilly temperatures, therapeutic hypothermia is a hot topic in the medical world, with numerous published studies and trials in the works, all trying to buy trauma patients an increased chance of recovery on the surgeon's table. Bradford says that SpaceWorks has been paying close attention to the studies coming out of the medical world, and that they think therapeutic hypothermia could be used safely on interplanetary flight, once some of the medical concerns of such an endeavor are studied and addressed.

One of the biggest issues facing human stasis using therapeutic hypothermia involves the simple fact that the method has only been tested in people who have been severely injured. "Nobody has done this on a healthy person," Bradford says, making it hard to isolate what benefits or problems the method could pose for astronauts in peak condition. Not only that, but the longest medical trials of therapeutic hypothermia have only lasted for 14 days, and a mission to Mars will take at least 180 days for a one-way journey.

Medical Concerns

Some of the other medical questions that therapeutic hypothermia faces:

- Cognitive function—How will being unconscious for six months affect the human brain, and how long will recovery take? "Is it going to be a couple hours, a couple days?" Bradford says, adding: "We'd like to measure how well you can perform when you get there." A recovery time on the scale of months would obviously be problematic. Bradford says that initial results from case studies showed that some patients who underwent therapeutic hypothermia actually performed better cognitively after the procedure than before. Then again, before the procedure, those patients were severely injured, so it's hard to say how astronauts would react.

Human Hibernation During Spaceflight

Suspended animation, the ability to set a person's biological processes on hold, has long been a staple of science fiction. Interest in the field blossomed in the 1950s as a direct consequence of the Space Race. NASA poured money into biological research to see if humans might be placed in a state of artificial preservation. In this state, it was hoped, astronauts could be protected from the dangerous cosmic rays zapping through space. Sleeping your way to the stars also meant carrying far less food, water and oxygen, making the ultimate long-haul flight more practical.

One recipient of that funding was a young James Lovelock. The scientist would dunk hamsters into ice baths until their bodies froze. Once he could no longer detect a heartbeat, he would reanimate them by placing a hot teaspoon against their chest (in later experiments, Lovelock warmed to the space-age theme by building a microwave gun out of spare radio parts to more gently revive his test subjects). These experiments on the flexibility of life would set him on the path to his most famous work, the "Gaia hypothesis" of the world as a living super-organism.

Frank Swain, "Human Hibernation:
Secrets Behind the Big Sleep," BBC, May 6, 2014.

• Muscle atrophy and bone loss—Staying in shape is hard enough for astronauts and cosmonauts who are awake. But add being completely sedentary to a weightless environment and the threats of muscle atrophy and bone loss become much more severe. To counter the physiological effects, Bradford says that astronauts in stasis will be treated with drugs to counter the bone loss, and their muscles will be given an electrical workout, stimulated by small electrical impulses. "We can envision that you're constantly being exercised in this manner," Bradford says.

- Intracranial pressure—One of the more enigmatic challenges faced by long-term spaceflight projects is the effect of intracranial pressure on astronauts. Researchers have noticed that without gravity, fluids in the body tend to move toward the upper body, raising pressure in the skull and affecting vision. Bradford says that some medical studies have found that induced hypothermia can reduce cranial pressure in situations here on Earth, which gives him hope that it could have a beneficial impact on astronauts.

- Radiations—Exposure to radiation is a huge challenge to long-distance spaceflight, but Bradford hopes that stasis using hypothermia could reduce the risk. A summary of the proposed method from SpaceWorks says: "Testing in animals has shown that cancerous tumor growth and the effects of radiation are significantly reduced and slowed during the torpor state (on par with metabolic rate reduction)." In addition, the savings on mass (no living quarters, less food, etc.,) mean that a transport vessel using stasis could theoretically be heavily armored against radiation in a way that a larger vessel could not.

Bradford says that the next phases of research will involve longer term testing on animals, then humans, and eventually, humans in space—likely on the ISS [International Space Station]. He's optimistic that with all the ongoing medical tests on therapeutic hypothermia, a viable solution for the Mars mission will be available well before any Mars projects get off the ground. "A space application is just part of it. Instead of developing some niche technology, we're going to leverage something that's existing," Bradford says.

And, just for the record, unlike many science fiction plots where something goes wrong and the capsule containing the astronauts is left to float in space for centuries, if something were to go wrong on a Mars mission using stasis, the hibernation system would automatically shut off, waking the crew and allowing them to make necessary repairs.

"Additive manufacturing is fast becoming an indispensable component of the modern-day industrial process, especially for niche applications such as space."

3-D Printing Could Revolutionize Space Exploration

Mark Williamson

Mark Williamson is a writer for Engineering & Technology *magazine. In the following viewpoint, Williamson contends that the burgeoning industry of 3-D printing could change the way people work in space. Small tools and even spare parts produced through 3-D printing have already been used on spacecraft, he writes, and the future of the venture could possibly see the printing of entire spaceships. This, he says, will lower costs and make space exploration more efficient.*

As you read, consider the following questions:

1. What functions does Williamson say 3-D-printed parts perform during the prototype phase of machinery production?

2. According to the viewpoint, in what way does 3-D printing's use of materials help reduce production costs for parts?

3. How does Williamson say an aircraft nose radome benefits from being 3-D printed?

General techniques of additive manufacturing (what we now call 3D printing) have become common knowledge in the engineering community. But to most of us it means watching a desk-sized printer slowly extruding plastic to form a model toy, key fob or similar inconsequential item. The 'resolution' of the device tends to be poor, leading to visible stepping in curved surfaces.

Despite this impression, additive manufacturing is fast becoming an indispensable component of the modern-day industrial process, especially for niche applications such as space. In 2014, the International Space Station received its first experimental 3D printer, which immediately earned its keep by printing a spare part for itself. Later, after an astronaut mentioned he could do with a socket wrench, a design was quickly developed, transmitted to the station and produced in orbit.

While you could argue that the astronaut's plastic wrench was closer to a Christmas cracker toy than something an earthbound car mechanic would find in the toolbox, space hardware that owes its existence to additive manufacturing is currently speeding its way to Jupiter, the largest planet in the solar system. The material of choice is not plastic, but that stalwart of aerospace: titanium.

The company responsible for the early adoption of the technology is aerospace giant Lockheed Martin which, far from being in it for the novelty, is "streamlining satellite production with 3D titanium printing to lower cycle times and reduce cost". According to the president of Lockheed Martin Space Systems, Rick Ambrose, 3D printing can reduce production times from months to days: "it could take a year to build a propulsion system. But printing can reduce this to days or weeks".

The way the process works is explained in a Lockheed graphic entitled '3D Printing 101' (the number has nothing to do with George Orwell's famous room, but refers to introductory courses in further education), which describes it in five easy steps. 1. Load design data to the printer controller. 2. Load titanium powder into the printer and evacuate the chamber. 3. Wipe the powder across a platform and melt with an electron beam. 4. Lower the platform and repeat until the object is formed. 5. Cool the part and return excess powder to the hopper.

Material Benefits

Titanium, typically alloyed with other metals, is widely used in the aerospace industry, largely because of its relatively low density, which is key to saving weight. Typical space applications include brackets, thrust frames and other structural components. But 3D printers can use a variety of materials, which according to Lockheed Martin's senior vice president & chief technology officer, Ray Johnson, is "a big part of the benefit of this new way of production".

The company currently uses 3D printers in two main ways: for prototyping parts, using polymers, and for printing "flight-ready parts" in titanium, aluminum and Inconel. (Inconel is a trademarked nickel-chromium 'superalloy' well suited to the high-pressure and high-temperature environments of space exploration.)

Lockheed Martin Space Systems (LMSS) has produced more than 300 parts through additive manufacturing, Johnson says, "most of them used for prototyping during the development phase". Sometimes, he explains, the parts are used as a substitute for a flight component, to accelerate the build, "while we wait for the actual item to be delivered"; alternatively, they help to demonstrate new concepts as part of a transition from more traditional manufacturing methods.

Actual flight-model components built by LMSS include an Inconel pressure vent, used in the flight test of NASA's [National Aeronautics and Space Administration's] new Orion capsule on 5 December 2014, and a set of eight structural brackets on the Juno spacecraft, which is currently en route to Jupiter.

These may seem like minor parts, but Johnson confirms that the size of space-qualified parts is growing "from brackets the size of playing cards to propellant tanks printed by room-sized machines". It is this increase in component size that brings "significant savings", he adds. For example, satellite propellant tanks could take up to 21 months to produce with today's manufacturing methods, such as titanium forging, but additive manufacturing technology can reduce this "to less than six months, and with a cost saving of over 50 per cent".

In fact, titanium tanks are the most complicated items the company has produced so far. "It may sound simple—empty fuel canisters—but it's not," says Johnson. "These tanks operate in space under incredible internal pressure, and also heed to survive high-g[1] loading and other environmental stressors related to launch."

Thinking in 3D

While the evolutionary improvement of industrial processes to save time and money is embedded in engineering culture, so

---

1. In aeronautics, load factor is the ratio of an aircraft's lift to its weight, usually expressed in units called g (not to be confused with acceleration of gravity, which is also expressed in g units).

too is the desire to find different and better ways to do things. Today, we know them as disruptive technologies or disruptive innovations.

In addition to the evolutionary developments, LMSS is marrying precision modelling and simulation with additive manufacturing to create complex parts that are impossible to manufacture traditionally. According to Johnson, "features like durable lattice work, intricate textures and organic shapes are all possible".

He uses an antenna-reflector fitting as an example. Based on customary design and manufacturing processes, the part was evolved by gradually stripping away material to save weight, reducing the mass from 395 g [grams] to around 80 g in the process. However, by designing from scratch for additive manufacturing, the resultant part weighed only 40 g. "It looks less like the original part", he says, "but we don't care about the shape. It's the functionality that's important".

It also reinvigorates the design process itself, because engineers can concentrate more on the functionality of a part than its shape. To encourage this, LMSS deploys its design engineers to the factory floor to work side by side with manufacturing engineers and "learn what additive manufacturing is truly capable of", says Johnson. "This hands-on approach stimulates creativity and encourages our design engineers to think differently about their designs".

Dennis Little, vice president of production at LMSS, agrees. "Our experience has been that engineers depend heavily on the left side of their brains, the hemisphere that favours the logical, sequential and analytical. 3D models and designs engage the right side, the hemisphere responsible for more creative and holistic thinking. When our engineers engage both their left and right brain, we are realising geometrically complex designs, features and parts never seen before."

Johnson thinks additive manufacturing is "opening new doors where design engineers innately think in three dimensions" and boasts that the company's engineers can now print "nearly any component they conceive".

The technology is a "critical component of our end-to-end digital manufacturing environment", says Johnson, an environment the company calls its Digital Tapestry, since it "weaves together the entire product development life cycle, from conceptualisation to product realisation". The Digital Tapestry is designed to provide a "seamless digital environment" to keep the digital data "intact" throughout the process.

To make this work, not just for LMSS but across each of Lockheed Martin's business areas, the company has established a corporate production council composed of leading individuals from each of the areas, which range from defence to information systems. A potential challenge with any disruptive innovation is the transition from laboratory to production and thereafter to the marketplace. As new technologies arise, explains Johnson, qualification can be difficult and time-consuming. "We are addressing this by ensuring that all of our business areas have access to the same quality systems and machines".

The national organisation tasked with encouraging the adoption of additive manufacturing is America Makes. Its director Ed Morris puts the case succinctly: "3D printing is a game changer because it has a whole new set of rules. When you change the rules, you change the game". By way of explanation, he adds that since 3D printing uses only the material required for the finished part, it "radically reduces" both waste and production time "which combine to yield a lower product cost".

Johnson is equally effusive: "The next generation of engineers won't be limited to the constraints of machining-based manufacturing", he opines. "Additive manufacturing is a huge leap forward in our vision for the factory of the future."

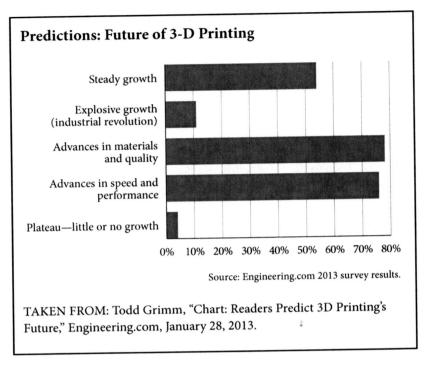

Predictions: Future of 3-D Printing

Source: Engineering.com 2013 survey results.

TAKEN FROM: Todd Grimm, "Chart: Readers Predict 3D Printing's Future," Engineering.com, January 28, 2013.

3D or Not 3D, That Is the Question

Technology is a subject often spoiled by hype: Remember the promise that nuclear electricity would be too cheap to meter? Or the expectation that man would be on Mars by the late 1980s? Or that computers and associated automation would allow us all to retire to a life of luxury?

What about 3D printing? What are we to make of news stories about printing food on the space station or the European Space Agency's concept for a 3D-printed moon base? Are these just examples of overhyped imaginative ideas, or grounded in reality? Perhaps a bit of both.

For a start, both ideas are dependent on what is known in the printer world as 'feedstock', in other words the stuff you feed your printer. In the first case, the feedstock must be an edible, presumably water-soluble substance, while in the second it is lunar regolith (soil or rock) converted into a form of 'lunar concrete'.

While it might seem cool to transmit the design for a candy bar to the ISS [International Space Station] and 'print it' in situ, instead of packing it onto a delivery capsule in the old-fashioned way, the mass of the feedstock and the water (and the mass of the printer) still has to be transported into orbit. And as for printing moon bases, isn't this just automated concrete laying? Admittedly, it's a challenging and clever system that can build a moon base without direct human intervention. But is this really 3D printing, or a misappropriation of an industry term?

The idea of building up a structure or component from stock material has been realised in the form of plaster-of-Paris models and fibre-glass boats for decades. In the aerospace industry, the technique was adapted to 'lay-up' composite structures for radomes and antenna reflectors. In parallel, computer-based design and computer-controlled machines have made the transformation of digital design files into products a daily reality. So is additive manufacturing simply an extension of CAD/CAM [computer-aided design/computer-aided manufacturing], a software-driven lay-up?

If the technology had peaked with the novelty key fob, or even the printed socket wrench, this might be a fair assessment, but consider Lockheed Martin's concept of 'pointwise composition control'.

The project started with a recognition that thermoplastic polymers should form the 'matrix' of future materials, because they were easily melted and could be deposited a layer at a time. They could also be compounded with a wide variety of reinforcing materials, such as carbon fibre and nanotubes, to control final properties. It didn't take long to realise that these new compounds used as feedstock for a 3D printer could produce "advanced design geometries that were not previously possible". Moreover, engineers could not only control the composition and functionality of a part, but also the composition at any location within the part. This is the nub of pointwise composition control.

A practical example that would benefit from the process is an aircraft nose radome, which typically houses a radar: The part must be light and strong, but its forward section must be transparent to radio waves. Another component printed to illustrate the potential and "capture the imagination of designers" features a circular gridded aperture at one end and a square grid at the other, with a colour transition from blue to green, the shade being an analogue for changing thermal or electrical properties.

But that's only the start of the concept, which foresees building an entire vehicle, a hand-launched UAV [unmanned aerial vehicle] perhaps, in a continuous process, with printed electronics embedded in the wings and solvent-resistant material for the fuel tank liners. A multi-axis robot coupled to feedstock mixing and blending equipment provides flexibility and access to a wider manufacturing area. Lockheed Martin says it's simply a matter of changing the properties of the feedstock on the fly.

For larger aircraft, the firm declares, you just need a larger factory and more robots, some floor-mounted, some on gantries, all working in concert. Perhaps printed rocket engines are closer than we think.

> "The specific benefits and potential scope of additive manufacturing remain undetermined, and there has been a substantial degree of exaggeration, even hype, about its capabilities in the short term."

3-D Printing Will Not Revolutionize Space Exploration in the Near Future

Dan Leone

Dan Leone is a staff writer for SpaceNews. In the following viewpoint, Leone writes that the National Research Council has refuted some of the hype surrounding the scientific capabilities of 3-D printing. The industry is more beneficial in the near term, the council has determined, and will more effectively prove its value by printing spacecraft parts on the ground, not entire craft or large craft parts in orbit. Leone reports that 3-D printing's long-term future in orbit has yet to be determined and further research and development is needed.

As you read, consider the following questions:

1. What does Leone say would be an obvious military application of 3-D printing?

2. What does Leone say is the obstacle to the development of ground-based 3-D printing systems?

3. For what operational spacecraft has the technology company Lockheed Martin used parts manufactured through 3-D printing?

Additive manufacturing, a trendy technique also known as three-dimensional [3-D] printing, probably will not spark an in-space manufacturing revolution any time soon, according to a report published July 18 [2014] by the National Research Council's (NRC) [Aeronautics and Space] Engineering Board.

"The specific benefits and potential scope of additive manufacturing remain undetermined, and there has been a substantial degree of exaggeration, even hype, about its capabilities in the short term," the NRC's Committee on Space-Based Additive Manufacturing wrote in its report, "3D Printing in Space."

The committee, which despite its cautionary tone maintained that 3-D printing could one day revolutionize the design of space hardware, prepared its report at the request of NASA [National Aeronautics and Space Administration] and the U.S. Air Force—groups that are not likely to begin printing entire spacecraft on orbit until "substantially in the future," the panel concluded.

Although there are obvious military applications, including on-orbit manufacture of satellite components, the NRC committee said human spaceflight stands to benefit most from in-space 3-D printing in the near term. That presents both obvious opportunities for NASA to test the technology at the

International Space Station [ISS] and obvious obstacles to industry investment, the panel said.

"Because some of the most obvious applications are for human spaceflight, the government cannot expect private industry to sponsor space-based additive manufacturing on its own," the panel said.

Still Earthbound

While the aerospace industry has made "extensive" investments in ground-based additive manufacturing, the NRC found no clear profit motive that would persuade manufacturers to pay out of their own pockets to develop the automated robotic systems required to evolve ground-based 3-D printing systems into useful on-orbit printing stations.

When additive manufacturing finally does migrate into orbit, it "is likely to have a significant impact on crewed space operations," the committee concluded. NASA is looking to get the ball rolling this year by sending a small 3-D printer provided by Made in Space of Mountain View, California, to the International Space Station aboard a Space Exploration Technologies Corp. [SpaceX] cargo resupply mission slated to launch Sept. 12.

NASA wants to find out whether additive manufacturing can help astronauts make replacements for interior ISS components that fail on orbit. The committee endorsed NASA's soon-to-launch experiment, noting that 3-D printing "could reduce existing logistics requirements for the International Space Station and future long-duration human space missions."

Overall, however, the committee said ground-based additive manufacturing "has more immediate and long-term impacts to reduce cost and increase performance of space systems." Further, "[t]he committee notes that the value of this technology will be demonstrated in the nearer term at the component level rather than the manufacture of entire spacecraft," the report reads.

Indeed, spacecraft builder Lockheed Martin Space Systems is among those singing the praises of 3-D printing.

"It's not a fad," James Crocker, Lockheed Martin Space Systems' vice president and general manager for civil space, said during a media day at the company's Global Vision Center in Arlington, Virginia, in June. "One of the most powerful things I've seen in 3-D printing is in fact the ability to build things that could never be machined . . . lightweight, very strong structures. They almost look organic. Printed parts don't look anything like you'd think."

Lockheed has already fitted a number of operational spacecraft with printed parts, including NASA's Jupiter orbiter Juno, which launched in 2011 and is set to arrive at the gas giant in 2016.

Even the ventilation system for Orion, the crew capsule Lockheed is building for NASA for a pair of missions to lunar orbit scheduled for 2018 and 2021, contains a part printed in titanium, according to the company's Orion deputy program manager Larry Price.

Periodical and Internet Sources Bibliography

The following articles have been selected to supplement the diverse views presented in this chapter.

Mark Albrecht and Don Kerr	"The Time for a New, All-American Advanced Liquid Rocket Engine Is Now," *CQ Roll Call*, April 17, 2014.
Jim Cantrell	"How Did Elon Musk Learn Enough About Rockets to Run SpaceX? Jim Cantrell Answers," *Forbes*, July 16, 2014.
Paul Davies	"Are We Alone in the Universe?," *New York Times*, November 18, 2013.
Jeffrey Kluger	"Maybe We Really Are Alone in the Universe," *Time*, March 20, 2015.
Lucas Mearian	"How Astronauts 3D Printed a Wrench They Needed in Space," *Computerworld*, May 19, 2015.
Eric Metaxas	"Science Increasingly Makes the Case for God," *Wall Street Journal*, December 25, 2014.
Dave Mosher	"NASA's Plutonium Problem Could End Deep-Space Exploration," *Wired*, September 19, 2013.
Jeff Nesbit	"Alien Life on Europa? Funding Gap Means We May Never Know," Space.com, August 14, 2013.
Eric Niiler	"Hibernation for Humans May Not Be a Pipe Dream Forever," *Washington Post*, April 13, 2015.
Richard Obousy	"Nuclear Propulsion for Solar System Domination," Discovery News, April 30, 2013.
Sarah Zhang	"We're Running Out of the Nuclear Fuel That Powers Space Travel," Gizmodo, December 2, 2014.

For Further Discussion

Chapter 1

1. Nelson Bridwell writes that humanity should begin preparing to vacate Earth for outer space in case of any unexpected cataclysms such as disease or comet strikes. Outer space, he believes, is the human race's ultimate destiny. Is Bridwell's advice practical? Should preparing for eventual disaster be a priority now, or do certain other issues take precedence? Explain your reasoning.

2. CJ Miozzi believes the National Aeronautics and Space Administration (NASA) should receive more funding both for the inventions that incidentally result from its projects and for space exploration itself. Do you think these are good reasons to increase NASA's funding? Are accidental innovations and space discovery worth billions of dollars of government money? Explain your reasoning.

3. Adam Rogers believes research into space tourism should be abandoned in favor of sparing the lives of those who may be killed in flight tests. Is he correct that human risk should make space-tourism enthusiasts give up their plans? Should the achievement of opening outer space for tourism be expected to carry inherent dangers with it? Explain.

Chapter 2

1. Louisa Preston writes that to alleviate the world's overcrowding, humans should begin planning to live on Mars, where they can cultivate vibrant plant ecosystems that will help them live. Do you think this plan will be practical or affordable by the year 2050, the year Preston says the world population will increase to eight to ten billion

people? Do other options exist to solve Earth's overcrowding aside from establishing a Mars colony? Explain.

2. Evan Ackerman argues that large floating cities in blimps should be installed in Venus's hospitable atmosphere to learn more about the planet. People could also live in these cities permanently. Do you think the opportunity to study Venus while moving a large group of people onto the planet is proportionate to the enormous costs that would be involved in the effort? Would this scientific advancement justify the multiyear, multibillion-dollar research and development project it would take to accomplish it? Why, or why not?

Chapter 3

1. Andrew L. Peek believes governments can encourage the private space industry by diplomatically protecting their space property claims in exchange for a share in private space technology. Do you think introducing property rights to outer space is a good idea? Is it the future of private space exploration, or will it only expand formerly earthbound international conflicts into space? Explain your reasoning.

2. Erin Wallace argues that NASA should receive more federal funding so it can continue demonstrating American scientific achievement and satisfying human curiosity. Do you think these reasons are valid enough to justify increasing NASA's funding? Should practical concerns such as finances be overshadowed by idealism? Why, or why not?

3. Michael Conathan writes that the federal government is unfairly devoting more money and time to space exploration than to ocean research. Which industry do you think is more important for humanity: exploration of space or

exploration of the oceans? Which of these arenas do you think holds more potential for beneficial scientific discoveries? Explain.

Chapter 4

1. Karl Grossman believes nuclear energy should not be used to power spacecraft, as any accident aboard a nuclear craft in space could trigger widespread devastation on Earth. Nuclear energy supporters claim, however, that the fuel, if used safely, would prove highly efficient for powering craft far into space. Is Grossman correct that the high risk of nuclear catastrophe should totally preclude using nuclear energy to power rockets? Or should it simply mean that greater care must be taken to ensure the safety of nuclear-powered spacecraft? Explain.

2. Stephen Morgan believes the existence of life-forms in extreme conditions on Earth signals that alien life-forms could live on other planets. Do you agree with his argument? Why, or why not? Explain.

3. Matt Williams writes that astronauts should use induced human hibernation to travel to Mars. So far, however, the method has been used only to save the lives of trauma patients, and its effects on healthy humans are currently unproven. Do you think testing such technology on astronauts in orbit is a worthwhile risk? Is human interplanetary travel scientifically beneficial in that it encourages the advancement of such new technologies? Explain.

Organizations to Contact

The editors have compiled the following list of organizations concerned with the issues debated in this book. The descriptions are derived from materials provided by the organizations. All have publications or information available for interested readers. The list was compiled on the date of publication of the present volume; the information provided here may change. Be aware that many organizations take several weeks or longer to respond to inquiries, so allow as much time as possible.

Blue Origin

21218 Seventy-Sixth Avenue South, Kent, WA 98032
(253) 437-9300
website: www.blueorigin.com

Blue Origin is an American aerospace manufacturer founded in 2000 by Amazon.com founder and chief executive officer Jeff Bezos. The corporation intends to make outer space available to private individuals by developing safe, affordable spaceflight technologies. Blue Origin's main achievement is its *New Shepard* vehicle, a reusable rocket with attached spacecraft that the company continues to test in pursuit of its larger mission. Blue Origin maintains an online press page of news articles, press releases, and blog posts about the company's recent activities. Article titles include "Blue Origin Completes Acceptance Testing of BE-3 Engine for New Shepard Suborbital Flight" and "ULA and Blue Origin Announce Partnership to Develop New American Rocket Engine."

Cato Institute

1000 Massachusetts Avenue NW
Washington, DC 20001-5403
(202) 842-0200
website: www.cato.org

The Cato Institute is a libertarian think tank cofounded by business magnate Charles Koch in 1977. It espouses the principles of limited government and maximized civil liberties for all Americans. Though it most frequently criticizes political decisions that affect the freedoms of American citizens, the Cato Institute has also commented upon the operations of the National Aeronautics and Space Administration (NASA), specifically its receipt and usage of government funds. For many years, Cato has called for an end to American taxes paying for a space program that it says offers American citizens no tangible benefits. The institute also has called for the privatization of NASA. Articles and commentaries on how Cato views NASA can be accessed on its website. Titles include "Space Program Was Our Biggest Bridge to Nowhere" and "Don't Lavish Funds on NASA."

Christa McAuliffe Space Education Center
95 North 400 East, Pleasant Grove, UT   84062
(801) 785-8713
e-mail: spacecenter@alpinedistrict.org
website: www.spacecenter.alpineschools.org

Established in 1990, the Christa McAuliffe Space Education Center utilizes simulation to give students a realistic and exciting space experience. The simulators provide students with insight into spaceflight, particularly the challenges of being an astronaut aboard space vehicles. The center runs a highly regarded summer space camp for students all over the world and offers classes and field trips during the school year. The center's website features curriculum information for teachers who are interested in instructing students in space and space exploration. Documents such as "Crew Positions Form" and "Ambassador Letters" are designed to enhance students' camp experiences of simulating that they are traveling into space.

Mars Society
11111 West Eighth Avenue, Unit A, Lakewood, CO   80215
(303) 980-0890
e-mail: info@marssociety.org
website: www.marssociety.org

The Mars Society is a nonprofit organization dedicated to the human exploration and settlement of Mars. The group fosters public outreach on this subject, lobbies for government-funded research on Mars, and facilitates private-sector funding and involvement in Mars exploration. Another mission of the Mars Society is to develop the Mars Analog Research Station program, which was created to provide useful field research facilities for NASA and other space organizations interested in spaceflights to Mars. The Mars Society's website hosts an education page featuring the blog *Red Planet Pen*, which discusses the settlement of Mars and society activities. The site also features a press page, which collects news articles from various sources. Article titles include "The Rocky Road to Space Funding Through Crowdsourcing" and "Year-Long Mock Mars Mission Picks Semifinalists for Canadian Arctic Crew."

National Aeronautics and Space Administration (NASA)

300 E Street SW, Suite 5R30, Washington, DC   20546
(202) 358-0001 • fax: (202) 358-4338
website: www.nasa.gov

The National Aeronautics and Space Administration (NASA) is a US federal government agency that operates the American space program while performing aerospace research. It was created in 1958 partially as a response to the space achievements of the Soviet Union, against which the United States was then competing in the Space Race portion of the Cold War. Although NASA's manned space shuttle program ended in 2011, the agency still operates numerous space exploration missions using satellites, rovers, and other robotic spacecraft. NASA regularly publishes space-related educational materials for students from kindergarten to college. Informational documents include titles such as "Aerodynamic Forces" and "Exploration: Solar System," among many others. These publications can be accessed online.

National Space Society (NSS)

PO Box 98106, Washington, DC   20090-8106
(202) 429-1600
e-mail: nsshq@nss.org
website: www.nss.org

The National Space Society (NSS) is an independent non-profit organization devoted to facilitating the human settlement of space and space exploration. The NSS lobbies Congress and raises funds to support its policies and advance legislation and policy pertaining to its goals. The society publishes *Ad Astra* magazine, a quarterly publication that covers subjects relevant to space exploration and settlement. The society's website also features a document page containing statements of society objectives, information on space colonization, and facts about society membership. These documents include titles such as "The Barriers to Space Settlement" and "NSS Strategic Plan."

Planetary Resources

6742 185th Avenue NE, Redmond, WA   98052
(425) 336-2448
e-mail: resources@planetaryresources.com
website: www.planetaryresources.com

Planetary Resources is an American aerospace company founded in 2010 that intends to build up Earth's natural resources for human space travel by mining valuable materials from asteroids. To do this, the company has worked to build safe, efficient, reusable spacecraft for the charting of asteroid paths and the eventual mining of these space rocks' minerals. Planetary Resource's main accomplishment in this field is its Arkyd telescope, designed to search for viable asteroids in near space. Planetary Resources hosts a press page on its website, featuring blog posts, press releases, and links to news articles. These articles include titles such as "The Space Rock Race: Mining Asteroids" and "Meet the Entrepreneurs at the Forefront of the Space Race."

The Planetary Society

60 South Los Robles Avenue, Pasadena, CA   91101
(626) 793-5100 • fax: (626) 793-5528
e-mail: tps@planetary.org
website: www.planetary.org

The Planetary Society is a membership organization made up of scientists, astronauts, entrepreneurs, educators, policy makers, students, business leaders, and space enthusiasts. It is recognized as one of the largest public space exploration organizations worldwide. The society advocates for sound space policy and space exploration, including a mission to Mars. The Planetary Society also focuses on education about space exploration. The organization's website features materials about space for both children and adults, including blog posts such as "5 Steps to Preventing Asteroid Impact" and "SpaceX Rocket Breaks Apart En Route to International Space Station."

Space Exploration Technologies Corporation (SpaceX)
1030 Fifteenth Street NW, Suite 220E
Washington, DC   20005-1503
(310) 363-6000
website: www.spacex.com

Space Exploration Technologies Corporation (SpaceX) is a private American aerospace manufacturing company founded in 2002 by South African–born entrepreneur Elon Musk. The company intends to reduce the costs of space exploration by engineering reusable rockets, which it has used to fulfill contracts with NASA to transport cargo to the International Space Station. SpaceX's ultimate goal, however, is to use its efficient technology to land people on Mars in hopes that humans will eventually become an interplanetary species. Press releases, announcements, and links to news articles about SpaceX can be found on its website. These articles include titles such as "SpaceX's 'Grasshopper' Reusable Rocket Prototype Makes Highest Flight Yet" and "Elon Musk's Mission to Mars."

Virgin Galactic
65 Bleecker Street, 6th Floor, New York, NY   10012
(212) 497-9050
e-mail: virgingalactic@virgingalactic.com
website: www.virgingalactic.com

Virgin Galactic is an aerospace technology company founded in 2004 by British entrepreneur Richard Branson, founder of the conglomerate Virgin Group. Virgin Galactic's primary mission is to revolutionize human spaceflight by developing the industry of space tourism. Through the engineering of its own spaceplanes, the company ultimately hopes to be able to fly people to space for recreation, allowing them to experience weightlessness and witness the sights of planetary orbit before returning to Earth. Virgin Galactic publishes fact sheets on its missions and technology, some of which are "Virgin Galactic Vehicle Fact Sheet" and "Galactic at a Glance."

Bibliography of Books

Mark Albrecht

Falling Back to Earth: A First Hand Account of the Great Space Race and the End of the Cold War. Lexington, KY: New Media Books, 2011.

Buzz Aldrin and Leonard David

Mission to Mars: My Vision for Space Exploration. Washington, DC: National Geographic, 2013.

Christopher Barnatt

3D Printing: The Next Industrial Revolution. Seattle, WA: CreateSpace, 2013.

Lee Billings

Five Billion Years of Solitude: The Search for Life Among the Stars. New York: Current, 2014.

Arlin Crotts

The New Moon: Water, Exploration, and Future Habitation. New York: Cambridge University Press, 2014.

Margaret Lazarus Dean

Leaving Orbit: Notes from the Last Days of American Spaceflight. Minneapolis, MN: Graywolf Press, 2015.

Chris Hadfield

An Astronaut's Guide to Life on Earth: What Going to Space Taught Me About Ingenuity, Determination, and Being Prepared for Anything. New York: Little, Brown and Company, 2013.

Brian Harvey

China in Space: The Great Leap Forward. New York: Springer, 2013.

Rick Houston	*Wheels Stop: The Tragedies and Triumphs of the Space Shuttle Program, 1986–2011.* Lincoln: University of Nebraska Press, 2013.
Chris Impey	*Beyond: Our Future in Space.* New York: W.W. Norton & Company, 2015.
Chris Impey and Holly Henry	*Dreams of Other Worlds: The Amazing Story of Unmanned Space Exploration.* Princeton, NJ: Princeton University Press, 2013.
Marc Kaufman	*First Contact: Scientific Breakthroughs in the Hunt for Life Beyond Earth.* New York: Simon & Schuster, 2011.
W. Henry Lambright	*Why Mars: NASA and the Politics of Space Exploration.* Baltimore, MD: Johns Hopkins University Press, 2014.
John S. Lewis	*Asteroid Mining 101: Wealth for the New Space Economy.* Moffett Field, CA: Deep Space Industries Inc., 2015.
Rob Manning and William L. Simon	*Mars Rover Curiosity: An Inside Account from Curiosity's Chief Engineer.* Washington, DC: Smithsonian Books, 2014.
Carolyn Collins Petersen	*Astronomy 101: From the Sun and Moon to Wormholes and Warp Drive, Key Theories, Discoveries, and Facts About the Universe.* Avon, MA: Adams Media, 2013.

Claude A.
Piantadosi

Mankind Beyond Earth: The History, Science, and Future of Human Space Exploration. New York: Columbia University Press, 2013.

Mary Roach

Packing for Mars: The Curious Science of Life in the Void. New York: W.W. Norton & Company, 2010.

Dirk
Schulze-Makuch
and David
Darling

We Are Not Alone: Why We Have Already Found Extraterrestrial Life. Oxford, England: Oneworld Publications, 2010.

Erik Seedhouse

Suborbital: Industry at the Edge of Space. New York: Springer, 2014.

Erik Seedhouse

Virgin Galactic: The First Ten Years. New York: Springer, 2015.

Michael G. Smith

Rockets and Revolution: A Cultural History of Early Spaceflight. Lincoln: University of Nebraska, 2014.

Neil deGrasse
Tyson

Space Chronicles: Facing the Ultimate Frontier. New York: W.W. Norton & Company, 2012.

Ashlee Vance

Elon Musk: Tesla, SpaceX, and the Quest for a Fantastic Future. New York: Ecco, 2015.

Roger Wiens

Red Rover: Inside the Story of Robotic Space Exploration, from Genesis to the Mars Rover Curiosity. New York: Basic Books, 2013.

| Jan Zalasiewicz and Mark Williams | *Ocean Worlds: The Story of Seas on Earth and Other Planets.* New York: Oxford University Press, 2014. |

Index

N